T0129900

Mankiya

Mankiya

Mary: Her Story

A Memoir

Written by
Vee Konkin

MANKIYA
A MEMOIR

iUniverse books may be ordered through booksellers or by contacting:

iUniverse
1663 Liberty Drive
Bloomington, IN 47403
www.iuniverse.com
1-800-Authors (1-800-288-4677)

ISBN: 978-1-5320-2144-2 (sc)
ISBN: 978-1-5320-2145-9 (e)

Library of Congress Control Number: 2017905494

Print information available on the last page.

iUniverse rev. date: 05/19/2017

Contents

This book is a biography about my aunt Mary. I wrote this for my daughter because she was always Mary's favorite great-niece. It is also for her husband so that he can understand where she learned some of her silliness. This is also for my sister, all my nieces and nephews, my great-nieces and great-nephews, and my great-great-nieces and great-great-nephews. To all my aunt's friends and their children, who often wondered about her but were too polite to ask; this will answer a lot of questions.

Preface

Since I could remember, I was very curious about my aunt Mary. She had many stories to tell her nieces and nephews. I enjoyed staying with her and my grandparents, even if it was to get away from my two older siblings, who were ten and eight years older, respectively. I thought they made my life miserable. I will not deny they spoiled me, and I let them. I always told my aunt that when I learned to read and write, I would write a book about her. Since I was nine years old, as I listened, I would write little notes and file them away in a little wooden cigar box. The box got filled, but I had no story. I worked and had little time to write. I told my aunt I would write when I retired and had nothing to do.

Her remark was "You will not remember me. Never mind. Write my story."

Long after she passed away, to prove her wrong, one day I got out the little box and sorted out my notes. I'd kept track of dates, people, and places. To tell you the truth, I did not know where to start. I wrote people's names that I changed, as well as places. I did not check the dates; some may not be accurate or the most exact. Most of the people were not real. I changed a few episodes to keep things interesting. This was based on her life and how she solved her problems. These are her memories as they were told to me over the years.

It is a story about her sad and happy times. She was a kind, lovable lady and would help anyone and everyone.

It is about experimental grafting, doctoring, and midwives of the early days.

This story is about communal living and hate, jealousy, and greed.

I thought I had a lifetime to write, in my later years when I got old. There was so much to see and do, and so many places to go to, like France, Spain, Portugal, the Caribbean Islands, Alaska, Canada, and the United States of America. There were so many places to go to, and so many friends with whom to spend time. My lifetime was going too quickly. I had to make time to write this because I was now retired and might not have much time. So, here it is. It's too bad Aunt Mary cannot read this.

Acknowledgments

I would never have written this without encouragement from my spouse and my daughter. I give a special thank-you to the people from iUniverse. To Dianne and Tammy, for encouraging me to continue and keep on. To Katie, a special thank-you for your patience and perseverance, and for helping me with all my mistakes. Without you, this would never have been written.

Thank you to Denis, my computer guru, and his wife.

Thank you to my spouse for his patience.

Introduction

This story is about the late 1800s and early 1900s. Immigrants came to settle in Canada; in this case, it was pacifists from Russia. With the help of Leo Tolstoy, the Quakers, and the Canadian government, the settlers went first to Cyprus. Because of poor nourishment, many lost their lives. The survivors came to the territories of Canada, now known as provinces. They worked hard, first building little hovels made of turf and sod; log structures were built later. All the work had to be done with bare hands. All the fields were dug manually, and after a day's work, they still had time to sing. They were allotted land if they wanted to stay in Saskatchewan or Alberta. Some wanted to live in communes, so they moved to the southern part of British Columbia, where they lived the communal life until 1955; then they had to buy the land.

They were known as the Orthodox Doukobour, not to be mistaken for the Sons of Freedom, who were the breakaway group. They did not reside in the same area, and there was some discord between the groups; there were many hard feelings between parents, children, and other relatives because they all believed differently. The Orthodox were peaceful, God-fearing people. The Sons of Freedom would go to meetings, disrobe, and burn homes. Most had no respect for Canadian laws. They had their children forcibly removed from their homes because they would not let them go to school.

Many of the Doukobours left the communal living to be in their own homes and believe in different religions. Many still live in the southern British Columbia area. They are now doctors, lawyers, and teachers, and many have prestigious positions. They are no different from other Canadians.

From Russia

It was 1895. We were on our way to Canada, wherever that may be. The big ship that we boarded in Batumi was rocking back and forth. I think most people were sleeping, some rather fitfully; I heard snoring and groaning. Farther away I heard people crying, and someone prayed out loud. The trunk with our belongings was sliding back and forth, sometimes close to me, forcing me to go closer to my sister Nellie, who was sleeping next to our mother, Axoota. Then it was our father, Wasa; our paternal grandparents, Hryna and Misha; and two teenage daughters, my aunties Dasha and Molasha. All were sound asleep—except me.

I tossed and turned and could not sleep, so I decided I would go exploring. I was not able to do so before; I had to stay by my parents' side or hold my sister's hand, which she was not anxious to do.

It was a stormy night: lightning flashed, and the thunder and rain came. I could see where to go: up the ladder and through the hatch. I had a hard time lifting it because it was so heavy, and I found myself on the wet deck. I tried to get out of the rain and edged along the wall of the cabin, behind coils of wet, smelly rope. There was a dry spot and a piece of canvas that covered a pile of rope. I hunkered down and peeked out as a wave hit. I covered up more and peered out. The ship rocked and rolled in the vast ocean. This was so exciting and adventurous! I made out the water, but only when the lightning lit up everything. This was the largest amount of water I had ever seen in my six years of life. It was an exciting new experience: a beautiful lightning storm.

As I sat in my little hiding space, behind some rolls of large rope covered with a large piece of canvas, I managed to stay dry. I could hear one of the deckhands singing in a very cheerful voice.

I recalled my past, as far back as I could remember.

The Village

I was born on a bright summer day, on June 14, 1889. I was a cute, chubby, blue-eyed, blonde-haired girl. I was the second girl in the family. Apparently there were two boys, and the first born was Wasil, who died at birth. Then there was Nicola, who died before he reached age one. My parents were trying for another boy, when I came along. But there I was, cute as a button.

I was two years old, and my sister, Nellie, was eight then. I tagged along behind her wherever she went in our little village in Russia. Everyone knew each other, and one could not get lost.

Koodrick was our cute but funny dog. He was short-legged and black with two brown spots over his eyes and a little white fur on his neck. He would be right behind us wherever we went.

Life was uneventful, living in a quiet, peaceful village in the beautiful countryside. The elders tended to fields, gardens, chickens, cows, sheep, and whatever else they had. Of course, the children also had small chores. Mine was to feed Koodrick. I guessed that was why he loved me: I was the food source.

One evening when we should be sleeping, we could

hear the adults talking about going to war. All seemed against it—the firearms and the army. Our father's brother, Uncle Soma, came one evening and announced that he had joined the army and was going to Moscow for training. Everyone cried. I could not see why everyone was so sad. I was five years old and did not know about armies or wars.

One night, out of our window we could see a big fire. All the men gathered on the hill above the village and burned all their guns, protesting against going to war because it was against their religion. It was 1895.

Then one evening, a meeting was called at the village meeting hall. Leo Tolstoy and the Quakers were helping people in our village to immigrate to Canada. The Canadian government had allotted land they could farm. We were told to leave Kavkaz. We had to leave Russia because the men refused to go to war and to carry guns. I knew they burned them and did not have any.

We packed and loaded whatever belongings we could get into a trunk, tried to tie furniture to the edge of the wagon, and had many satchels packed with food and clothes. Anything we could carry, we did. I carried my doll, Kukla. It was bad enough leaving the village, Uncles Misha and Nicola, and their families. My cousins got to keep Koodrick—how I cried. As we walked, I looked back every chance I got, until through my teary eyes, I could no longer see the buildings and the people waving good-bye. I could no longer see Koodrick.

This was a big adventure for a little girl who had never been out of the village. People were everywhere as we went along, with more joining us from different villages.

Many cried, some sang psalms, and others prayed. It was a sad time. We had cows tied to the wagons to provide us with milk, as well as chickens in wooden crates for eggs.

We walked and walked. I thought I would drop because I was so tired, as were the animals. I missed Koodrick and could not understand why I could not take him.

We stopped at nights and ate whatever our mother prepared. She was so tired, and so Nellie and I helped as much as we could. Then we spread the thick, wool-filled comforters on the ground under or beside the wagons, and we fell into an exhausted but troubled sleep. The cool mornings came too soon, and after a quick breakfast, we were on our way again. Oh, how I missed the peaceful life of the village. How I missed my cousins and Koodrick.

We walked for days and slept many nights. One seemed to be a continuation of another, and it was very exhausting. We went through small villages, where more people joined us. Everyone was so sad, and in a few days, the newcomers were as tired as the rest of us.

One night we stopped, and a group of people speaking a strange language came to talk to us and inquire as to where we were going. We understood some of the words, and we were told they were Armenians. They soon left, and we continued on our journey.

One afternoon, all the sky turned black, and the wind started to blow. There was no place to take shelter except under the wagons. I thought I was going to get blown away. I thought Kukla was going to get blown away, and I hid her under my arm and hung on to her for dear life; it seemed she was all I had. That night the wind blew, there was thunder and lightning, and the rain pelted us.

I thought I would drown, and the animals were skittish and unsettled. By morning the storm blew over, and the sun was again shining. Soon we got on our way, all dry, and we got warmer as the day wore on.

Teblis and Batumi

Finally, we came to a bigger village. I was told this was a town called Teblis. We rested for a few days, where we sold or gave away the oxen, the wagons, and everything we could not carry. We boarded a big, noisy train—something many of us had never seen before. I was excited by the experience of riding on these two ribbons of steel.

Soon we were in Batumi, which seemed even larger than Teblis. There were lots of water, large ships, and little boats and all kinds of interesting things to see in the harbor. People milled around everywhere. Merchants were selling all kinds of goods: fish, fruit, vegetables, and many things we had never seen or heard of. What fascinated me the most were those gooey-looking beans I saw people buying and chewing. The Cossack selling them asked if I would like to try one. Fascinated, I could only nod. I tasted it, and it was the sweetest thing I'd ever had in my life. Many years later, I learned it was a carob bean. We wandered from stall to stall. At one of the stalls, I was offered a clear crystal, glasslike substance on a string; it was rock candy. How I savored that—it was the best thing I'd ever eaten! I would suck on a crystal and then wrap the rest in a handkerchief and put it in my farteec pocket. (Farteec is the apron we wore over our long skirts.) The candy lasted for a long time.

This was where I had my first scary encounter with Osiya Trofeeminko. He was an older man with a gray beard and gray hair that was thin on top. He had bushy gray eyebrows that nearly covered his beady black eyes. He was always ringing his rough hands, and he had a snide grin with two front teeth missing. He was not a nice or kind man; I heard him swearing at his wife and at his only son, who looked like he was petrified of him and would hide behind his mother's skirt. All the older girls avoided Osiya. My sister Nellie told me not to be near him and not to be caught alone with him because he was a bad man.

In my inquisitive, childish trance, I wandered away from my mother. All at once, I felt these rough hands grab me and pull me behind a covered stall. I tried to scream, but a rough hand covered my mouth. The rough hands went to my legs, just up from where my stocking ended and my long bloomers started. I got even more scared when I looked up and saw those beady black eyes peering out from under his gray, bushy eyebrows. I bit down on the scaly, dirty hand. I must have bit hard enough for him to release his hold over my mouth, and I screamed as loud as I could while I kicked and fought.

All at once, this large figure loomed from in front of the stall. It was the Cossack who had given me candy. He hit Osiya, so hard that the man landed on the ground. The Cossack took me up in a gentle hold and ran to my mother. My mother was so happy to see me. For days I would not let go of her skirt, and once I peered out to see those beady eyes watching me. But these eyes were different, because one was hurt and black all around, and his face looked like it was scratched and bleeding in several spots. He was favoring his arm, which looked black and blue. My father and mother had a long discussion about this, and they told my sister, our aunts, and me to stay as far as possible from this perverted old man.

Finally the day came when a big ship came to port. It was the biggest boat I had ever seen. On the side was written *Lake Huron*. I listened. There was a lot of talking going on, but not much made sense to me. I was curious: who was Leo Tolstoy, who was Queen Victoria, who were the Quakers, and who were the pacifists in Canada? These people were all helping us to go to Canada. Where was Canada? Why were we going there? First this ship was going to Cyprus. Where was Cyprus? Why were we going there? It was not Canada.

All I got for an answer was that everyone was going there, and it would be our new home. In my childish ignorance, I was excited at this new experience, but in the back of my mind, I still longed for the quiet village and my dog.

The day came when we were to board the big ship. All families were to board together and stay together. I was so frightened that I hung on to my mother's skirt. Up the gangplank we went; the water was dark and so far below us. When we got on board, there was a man writing down all our names. I said to myself, "Someday I will learn to write and read."

I was standing by the railing and glanced over the second rail. I could see the handsome Cossack who'd saved me from terrible Osiya. He waved, I waved back.

We were assigned places for our trunks and where to sleep. We ate meals prepared by our mothers, with food purchased at the stalls on the dock. We did not have cows for milk or chickens for eggs anymore, but we did have other food, including lemons for our tea and fresh oranges. I still had my sugar crystal candy in my pocket.

With a lot of smoke and a loud blow on a horn the ship pushed off from the dock. I jumped when I heard that loud noise. If the dock was crowded, the ship was even more so. Sometimes I felt like someone would squash me, but I was very excited. Some people looked up to the sky and said, "Hospadi blahaslavee," which meant "God Bless." Many people around me prayed, some quietly and some out loud. Many cried.

It started to rain, and so most of us went down the hatch. Some lay down to go to sleep, and many children and women cried. The men were trying to be brave, but a lot of them had tears in their scared eyes. The people around me all looked sad. Everyone was tired. My parents spread out blankets and were bedding down for the night, as were my sister and I. Pretty soon all were sleeping. This was my chance to sneak away and explore. All I could think of was breathing some fresh air, so up the ladder I went.

Wide Awake

What a rude awakening I had. One of the crew members whom I had seen on the deck earlier, grabbed me by the back of my coat and pulled me straight up from my hiding place behind the piles of smelly rope. He yelled at me. I believe he was scolding me for being on the deck by myself.

Amid this yelling and my crying, my father came to the rescue. With a strict scolding and a slight thump on the back of my head, he shoved me down the hatch, where the rest of the family was frantically looking all over for me. A lot of them were happy to see me, but some were very angry that I had brazenly disappeared and scared them. My mother was so happy to see that I was safe that she put her arms around me and sobbed. Even my sister gave me a hug.

I did not understand what all the excitement was all about. I must have fallen asleep and slept well all night long. The last thing I remembered was the beautiful lightning storm and thinking of our village. I hugged Kukla, my dolly, and smiled at everyone.

Everyone settled into life aboard the ship, cooking,

eating, and exercising when our turn came to go on the deck. We could not all go up at once, so we took turns.

I saw the crew member who had found me among the ropes, and he waved and smiled at me; he was not angry anymore. He said, "Hi, little girl."

I replied, "Hi."

That was my first word of English, and it sounded great. I was going to learn the new language. I was going to speak to everyone. I was thinking of learning Armenian, English, and reading and writing Russian, so I could write to my cousins in Russia. It seemed so far away.

Everyone sat around and some sang the old Russian hymns that they'd known since their childhood days. Most adults worried and wondered what was to become of them. Where would they live, and would they get enough food to eat? Would crops grow in Canada?

So This Is Cyprus

Soon we saw the port, and we landed on the island of Cyprus, at a place called Laranica. I learned we were now in Turkish territory. We unloaded all our belongings on the docks. Where were we going? There were many wagons drawn by horses, and they were different from oxen. They were large, beautiful animals with hair on their necks and long, swishy tails.

Some of our belongings were loaded on the wagons. We walked to a farm. Some people stayed at the first one we stopped at, but we continued on. It was so hot and humid, and the water we were drinking was not tasty, but we were thirsty, and so we drank it. We were so tired. Some people were dropping from exhaustion.

We reached a large farm, and some of the people in other groups stayed there. It was Pergamos, but we learned in the morning our family was to go to the next farm, which was a lot farther, and so we walked. I was so exhausted. A kindly man on horseback scooped me up and let me ride behind him on the horse; my mother was right there, so I felt safe. The ride relaxed my aching legs and feet.

We went on for days, but it seemed like weeks to many

of us. Some people died. Our neighbor Hreesha's wife, Haniya, died during the night. I woke to loud sobbing, and their three young children were crying as Hreesha tried to console them. We had to bury Haniya in a field. People said prayers and sang a few psalms, and the family threw handfuls of dirt into the grave. Then the body was covered up with the rest of the dirt. A few rocks were placed to mark the spot. This was my first experience with death and funerals, and I did not like it, but over the months I had to get used to it. A lot of people died.

We finally arrived in Athalassa, where we were to live—but no celo (village), and no houses. My father and grandfather dug out an area. This was where we lived, with trees and branches to cover the top, and we sort of settled in. Every day our parents tried to make it more livable, and every day there was something new, like a shelf, a table, and benches. There was a garden plot to be dug, and the women and children all joined in. Some parents had brought seeds from Russia, and they planted them. We worked and toiled every day.

The sun was so hot that we drank the rank-tasting water, and then we worked some more. Nighttime, was a blessing, and we dropped off to sleep. Before I knew it, it was morning and time to start a new day that was the same as the day before.

One day my father came home and said, "I have a job at the farm next to this one. It is an English lady who needs help with the chickens and the pigs."

He went to work the next day. He came home in the evening very tired but grinning from ear to ear. The nice lady had given him six eggs and a crock full of milk. My mother cooked over an open fire outside our makeshift house, making rice kasha with the milk. It tasted so good because we had not had milk for a long time. That night we went to sleep more contented.

Every day Papa went to work, and every day we worked harder. Grandpa, Grandma, my two aunts, my sister, and I would work in the garden and the fields. Mama did the washing and made sure we had clean clothes. These she would scrub in a wooden tub brought with us, rubbing the dirt spots on stones with lye soap also brought from Russia. Then she would throw them on the bushes to dry them. They smelled so good and were clean.

One day Papa brought butter, and one day it was wheat. Mama pounded the wheat between two rocks into a flour, and she made tasty meals like zateerke, a sort of noodle made with an egg and water, dried in the sun and boiled into a soup. She also made solamata, which was browned flour mixed into a paste with salt, a bit of the delicious butter, and water. We enjoyed the different things my mother made.

Some days Papa brought home cabbage, carrots, potatoes, turnips, and vegetables, which we had never before seen or heard of. At least we had something to eat. We would share with others who were less fortunate. In the meantime our gardens started to sprout. Soon we had vegetables too.

One day, I went to the farm where Papa worked. I had not seen anything so beautiful in my life. Green fields caught my eyes, and beyond that was short green grass. The beautiful white house looked so large and had porches all around it, along with windows and lacy curtains. Everything shone in the morning sun. All the buildings were very big. I thought Papa and his friends were so lucky to work there.

As we approached the house, a good-looking lady, the nicest I had ever seen, came onto the porch. She had a jug of yellow-looking water and glasses, and she handed everyone a glass filled with lemonade. It quenched my thirst and was sweet; I wanted more but did not ask. Papa had to clean the pig pens, so the pigs were chased into a smaller pen through a chute. Then all the pig droppings were shoveled out onto a wagon, to be taken to the fields and scattered to make things grow. I was told all this by Papa. It was a smelly job, and I could not help, so I wandered away.

As I rounded a little shed, there was a *woof*, and then another. I saw puppies, and a mama dog wagged her tail and was friendly looking. I got down on my knees and pet her soft, brown coat. The two little brown puppies were so cute and licked my face like Koodrick used to do. I cried and cried as the puppies licked and playfully chewed on me. I was happy and spent most of the time with the dogs. I loved them, and they loved the attention they got from me.

I heard the pigs squealing. Papa was herding them back through the chute and into the clean pen. He put a notched board into the fence as they went through; this board rubbed on their backs and pulled off some of the bristly hair. He removed the board once in a while and put the hair into a handkerchief. He had two piles of hair, one white and one black, when he finished with the pigs. These he tied into a knot and put it into his pocket. I asked him what that was for.

He answered, "You will see, later."

That day we went home loaded down with vegetables, eggs, and a piece of material. It was a pretty blue with tiny pink flowers on it and was so soft. The kind lady gave it to me and motioned it was to be made into a dress.

I went home happy that night. I showed the material to Mama, and she said there was enough there to make me a dress and a blouse for Nellie. I think my aunts were jealous. I was not happy with their jealousy; I loved them all just the same.

With the pig hairs Papa brought home, he made a brush, mounting them on a piece of leather and attached to a wooden top that he carved. It served well to brush stuff that adhered to our woolen clothes. A lot of our clothes were made from wool—hand-carded, spun, and then woven into cloth.

Life was hard on Cyprus. The heat was getting to many people, food was scarce, and many people went blind from improper nourishment. We were lucky to get eggs and milk given to us, to grow our own vegetables, and to be able to work hard in the gardens. All the women and children worked together. Even though I was little, I kept up with the older ones, both of my aunts and my sister.

During the night, I heard shouts and commotion outside of our little living quarters. One of our neighbors, Tanya, was having labor pains, so my mother went to help deliver her baby. Later, we went to see a cute tiny little baby girl. They called her Malenka, and she was so tiny. I did not recall seeing anyone so small. Tanya was not well, and so Mama took Tanya some of Mama's cooking. With the extra food, in a few days she felt stronger.

We heard that many of the people who went to a farm farther north were very ill, and many were dead. Some who stayed on the first farm were dead too. People were very ill and dying around us. Something had to be done. There was not enough food, there was poor drinking water, and the heat was getting to many. A lot of the older folks were in a weakened condition.

Thank goodness all our family was healthy enough. I always thought it was the extra food Papa brought home that kept us healthy. Any extra food we had, we shared with others who had none.

There was talk that we would have to go back to Laranica and board a ship to Canada. We all talked about the long walk there. Oh, how I dreaded the trek. I was going to miss the cute little puppies and going over to the nice lady's farm. I was getting used to this place, and I hated the thought of getting uprooted again. Grandpa told me not to worry; I was very young and would adjust to anything, anywhere I went.

One sunny day, we were told we were to leave in two days in order to get to the port and catch the ship going to Canada. The time came to trek to Laranica. It was such a long way to go.

I went with Papa to say good-bye to the nice lady and the cute dogs. How I wished I could take them all with me! The beautiful lady gave me a handkerchief, and I would treasure it forever. I cried all the way home. Papa tried to console me, but that made me cry even more. Why was life so unfair, so complicated?

The day came to go, and we walked and walked. We were so tired by evening. The daytime was so hot that people were dropping from exhaustion. Children cried, and grandparents cried and prayed. Some weakened folks died, to be buried in the fields with a small prayer and hardly a marker to note the spot. We went on until we reached the port.

Atlantic Ocean

The large ship, *Lake Huron*, was waiting. Food and provisions for the trip across the ocean were purchased on the docks by those who still had a few rubles left.

We went through the same routine as before. Families grouped together as we boarded the ship. A man sat and wrote down everyone's name. We were a lucky family: we were still here, and even if we were weak, we were still quite healthy. As we walked to our designated spots on the ship, I spotted the sailor who'd found me hiding on the deck that stormy night. I tried to hide behind Mama's skirt, but he saw me, smiled, and said hi. When I blushed, he gave a hardy laugh and sounded pleased to see me. I was so embarrassed, but I certainly was not going to sneak up on the deck at night anytime soon.

Around us were many familiar faces. A lot of people looked gaunt and thin, and many looked sick. Many had lost weight, to the point of looking like skeletons.

We got settled in our places and were extremely exhausted from the long journey and the heat; even if it was spring, it was getting very hot. I saw some of the children with whom I had previously been acquainted.

The following day, with a *ding-dong* of the ship's

bell and a loud whistle, we began our trip across the Atlantic Ocean to Canada. First we had to go through the Mediterranean Sea. There were spots where we were close to land, and it was very interesting. I listened very well, and we passed Malta, an island. Then we were north of the continent of Africa, a country called Egypt. As we continued, we passed Spain on the other side of the ocean. We went through a narrow passage where we could see land on both sides of the ship; one side was Spain, then Gibraltar, and on the other side was Morocco. Soon we lost sight of land, and all we had was water and more water.

The days seemed the same. We had our turns on the deck, we ate what Mama prepared, and we slept (most times fitfully). One evening before retiring, our family was taking its turn for a walk on the deck before going down to sleep. I heard music. A crew member was playing a funny, handheld, little metal thing. I stopped to look and listen with interest. He held it out for me to see and said, "This is called a mouth organ. It makes music. Can you dance?"

He got up and did a dance. I could do the Cossack dance, so I squatted and danced while he danced and played the mouth organ. The people who were on the deck watched and were very entertained; some danced, laughed, or clapped their hands.

My parents had walked on ahead of me, and suddenly they realized that I was not with them. They retraced their steps and saw that it was me They retraced their steps and saw that it was me who was creating the performance. They were very embarrassed, but I could not see why—I was having fun. I was given a talking to and was told not to do this again.

Grandpa made a few rules for me. No more dancing, especially to the music provided by the crew members. We had to join in our elders group in prayer, singing hymns and psalms. Occasionally they sang quick and happy songs, but not very often. That was fun, otherwise it was very boring.

It was a sad and long crossing to get to Canada, and I hated being confined to our family, who all kept an eye on me. I could not wander around the ship on my own.

As I listened to the older people talking, I learned 108 people had died in Cyprus; some were people I knew, but a lot were from other villages I had not even heard of. There were over one thousand making the trip to Canada. This trip was funded by Leo Tolstoy and the Quakers from England and the United States. Some of the conversation I overheard was interesting.

One day we were all on the deck and I saw a bird. Hopefully we were close to land. Papa said it was a good sign that we were. Soon there was a sighting of land, and it was exciting. We could see mountains in the distance, and soon we were able to make out big rocks and cliffs and trees, with birds flying everywhere. Then we had land on both sides of the ship, and I could see trees with needles and leaves; some trees and bushes had flowers on them. We were in the harbor of Quebec.

We had to meet with port authorities, as we were let off the ship, and all families were registered in a big book by a very serious-looking man. He wrote our names. My name officially was Mary (Mankiya was childish). He wrote down date of birth, where we were born, and where we were going.

Where *were* we going? Someone said Manitoba. Where was Manitoba? Grandpa told us it was a big territory of Canada. We were now in Canada, in the territory of Quebec. How knowledgeable Grandpa was. I thought that someday I would know everything like him. We stayed in groups, and I stuck close to our family. It was an exciting but scary time. It seemed like a big country, with lots of rivers, lakes, and mountains. We were going to the prairies, which were a flatland. I took it all in, and it was very interesting.

I asked many questions, and some answers my grandfather did not provide because he did not really know everything. *I'm going to learn and know everything someday,* I thought.

We were given lodging in a big hall. We had bread and different vegetables and cheese that was orange. I'd never eaten orange cheese, but it tasted good. In the morning there was milk and eggs to eat. If this was Canada, it was not at all bad!

We stayed in Montreal for a few days, and then we were escorted to the railyards. We were there to get on a train and go to our promised land. The big engine came chugging into the train station. It was steaming and was so loud that most little children hid behind their mothers' skirts, as I did, though I still peeked out because I was afraid I'd miss something. Pretty soon we got on the train, and families stayed together. We were assigned seats in close proximity of each other. My sister and parents kept an eye on me, as did my aunts and grandparents.

I got to sit by a window. It was interesting to look out at the hustle and bustle at the station. People were coming and going, and some of the ladies were dressed in pretty dresses and carried beautiful purses. Young children were around. I stared at them because they were dressed differently than we were. The girls had cute dresses, and some stuck their tongues out at me—that was not nice. Someday I would dress like them, but I would not stick my tongue out at anyone.

Soon the train let out a shrill whistle and started to move. We were off on another exciting journey. A man, called a conductor, came through the coach we were in, talked to all the passengers, and gave them a piece of paper. He said it was a ticket for the next train that we would be going to get on in Toronto to go on to Winnipeg, Manitoba. At last, our future home.

We traveled out of the city and into the countryside with lots of tree and bushes and animals. There were deer, as well as a few furry, big creatures called buffalo, I was told that soon we would be going alongside a lake, and it sure had a lot of water. I was tired and fell asleep.

When I awoke, it was starting to get dark, and I had to go relieve myself quickly. My mother took me down the aisle to the back of the coach. We went into a little cubicle that had a shiny white place to sit on and go to the toilet. Then I had to pull the handle, and everything fell down. I could see the ties and some of the rails. Other than the ship, that was my first experience with a toilet that was not outside. I went back to my seat and pressed my nose to the window until it got too dark to see. I again fell asleep.

At daylight, the conductor came through the train

and announced that we were in the city of Toronto. We left the train we were on and got on another one almost right away. I watched through the window and saw a lot of people at the station. A lot of women had beautiful clothes, shoes, and handbags that they carried. *Someday I will have all that,* I thought. *I am in Canada. I will have all that.*

We were off again and went by a lot of lakes, rivers, and mountains. Soon we were into flatter land and smaller mountains. We ate whatever food we had with us.

Not Manitoba

We travelled for two days to Winnipeg, Manitoba, and we did not get off the train there. I thought we were going to Manitoba, but we did not get off, not even to stretch our legs. Then three days passed, and on the fourth day, we reached our destination. There were no nice hills and no trees.

We were told we were in Yorkton, Saskatchewan. When we got off the train, the wind was blowing. The town was smaller than the other cities we had been in. We had to collect our belongings, small as they were, and carry everything. I still had Kukla, but I had to carry other things.

We spent a cold, miserable night in a building. Some ladies who spoke English gave us food to eat.

In the morning it was very cold and windy. After a breakfast of hard-boiled eggs and bread, we had to be on our way, because we had a long way to go.

Soon we were walking again. We had to go from Yorkton to places called Michada, Verigin, Kamsack, and Pelly, which was near the Manitoba border—and which was forty-five miles away. Good thing I was young and had strong legs.

There were a few trees, and a few people came out to see this strange group of new settlers as we walked to our new homes. Where were the houses? Where were the buildings? I was informed that there were no buildings, and that the men would build them.

I thought our previous walks were long, but this was longer, with cold winds one could not hide from. We kept on. Uncle George and his family stayed in Michada. Some people stayed in Verigin, and others continued to a place called Kamsack. Our family and a few others walked on to Pelly, close to the Manitoba border.

There was no shelter, and we slept huddled together to survive the nights. The morning brought us some sunshine and a bit of hope. Papa and Grandfather stepped off some land and said, "We will dig here and build a shelter to shield us from the wind." All morning we dug with one makeshift shovel and pieces of twigs; the children dug with their hands. Pretty soon a hole seemed to appear in the little hillside. Papa got big twigs and then smaller ones, put them over the hole, and got stronger ones for the front of the little hovel. That night, we slept out of the cold wind. Thank goodness we still had some of our wool blankets.

The next day, Papa and Grandfather got our only shovel and cut and dug up sod, chunks of grass that had grown together. This made our walls and a roof for our hut, but more branches were needed on the roof first. Our humble existence started in Pelly, Saskatchewan.

Our neighbors were a few miles down the road, and they were in the same predicament as we were. We helped each other, as we did in Cyprus. Soon we had a celo, a village. More people moved in closer and built little dwellings of wood and clay.

In our celo, we had people whom we knew from before, but there was one downfall: we had that nasty Osiya Treafeeminko and his wife. They had a son a year younger than I, and his name was Waskya. He was a nice enough boy, but we were afraid of his father, and so we avoided him too. He grew up to be a very lonely boy with a nasty father and a timid mother who seldom talked to anyone. We noticed she was covered with bruises many times, and we heard our parents saying, "Osiya beat her again. He probably beats Waskya too." We felt so sorry for Waskya, and after that we were nice to him and his mother.

We planted gardens with the seeds we'd brought from Russia and Cyprus, after digging with sticks, hands, and whatever we had. Soon, some rain came, and gardens sprouted up. Our roofs leaked and continuously needed repair. Our dirt floors turned to mud many times.

Our papa somehow got a hand saw; he said he worked for it. He and Grandfather sawed boards, and soon we had a pile, with twigs in between to dry them out. Soon we had enough for a wall, and then another. Thicker boards were for the corners and something on which to put the boards. Pretty soon a house grew from the pile of boards.

We got three chickens. Papa brought them home one day, and two laid eggs every day, one every other day. Mama said to take no eggs for a while. Then one hen sat on the nest for tree weeks and hatched eleven little yellow chicks running after the hen. They were so cute! Soon they grew into brown-and-gray hens, and one turned out to be a big gray rooster.

We got food from our garden. Papa and the men in the celo helped each other with buildings and fields. Horses were soon acquired; before that, the ladies did a lot of plowing and most of the gardening.

I turned twelve years old. Mother had a new baby, and we called her Noora. We all loved her and took turns bouncing her on our knees. She hardly had a chance to cry, so my new sister never had a moment without someone looking after her. Papa and Mama were disappointed. Noora was not the son they desired, but they loved her all the same. We all loved her.

Life went on with years of hard work. No one had said it would be easy. There were many hard years of living on the bald prairies.

Some evenings when Papa was not too tired, he would read in Russian to us. Nellie and I learned the alphabet and were soon reading to Papa, and we learned to write in Russian. I finally wrote to my uncles in Russia, but I had a hard time getting anyone to take the letter to Yorkton to mail it; it needed stamps to go in the mail across the ocean. I finally did little chores to earn enough money for a stamp, four cents. I did not realize it was so hard to get four cents. I dug up carrots for one neighbor and looked after a colicky baby to get the money.

Love Happens

There were weekly meetings, as well as prayer meeting on Sundays, where the celo got together and socialized. Some of the young got married and started families; other youngsters made eyes at each other and smiled.

I went to visit my cousins and aunties in Kamsack, which was a bigger village. It was a long walk, and Nellie and Grandmother came. It was an interesting time, because Nellie was making goo-goo eyes at a nice-looking fellow, but she was told to behave because he was promised to Tatyana, a distant cousin of ours.

It was fun to be away from our parents, even if it was a disappointment to Nellie. She was older than me and had boys on her mind. I could not quite understand, so she told me some facts of life. She told me about love, marriage, and having children.

Aunt Dasha decided to marry Soma, who came over on a different ship from Russia. He was a very enterprising young man, and he had a small business buying and selling things in the town of Kamsack. Soma was very independent, and Grandmother was very worried about her daughter, but she and Grandfather thought it over and decided that it would be all right. Dasha and Soma got married, and we all celebrated. She had a few things in her much-treasured hope chest, like woolen sweaters, socks she had knitted, hand-embroidered shawls, and woolen skirts and blouses. I made her a towel and a small kerchief, which she put in her hope chest. She got married and went to live in the town of Kamsack. I wished it was me.

I met Vasyl Zubov, the light of my life, but we were too young. We would chase each other and laugh. I decided if I had to marry, it would eventually be Vasyl.

Love Happens to Nellie

A few miles down the road, there lived a Ukrainian family. The Kolosovs were Mike, Nada, and three good-looking boys. They were a hard-working family, as most people were in those days.

Nellie and I were supposed to be working, digging Seneca root. It grew wild on the flat prairie. It was sold to a man who bought it from us; it was used to make medication.

Instead, we decided to go for a dip in the water because it was a hot day. There was a spot in the little creek that made a neat swimming hole. As we neared the water, we heard laughter. It was the Ukrainian boys, and they were swimming in the nude. We crouched down and watched. We crawled back farther so as not to be seen.

Soon the boys got out of the water, got dressed, and left. We waited a long time to make sure they were gone. We took off our skirts and tops; being modest, we left on our camisoles and underpants. Then we slowly eased ourselves into the water. It was so cool and refreshing. Nellie swam and was a natural. I floated on my back, careful not to go out too far. We had a great time.

We could hear snickering from the deep grass—the boys were back. We panicked. What were we to do?

Finally the boys stood up and came toward us. Very shyly, they searched the ground because one of the boys had lost his knife. We understood their language a bit; some of it was similar to Russian. They found the knife and were ready to leave, but one was reluctant to go. He said his name was Andre, and he wanted to know our names. We stayed in the water up to our necks. I told him I was called Mariya, and my sister was Nellie. He said he would see us again, and then he ran to catch up to his brothers. Nellie said it was love at first sight, and she thought Andre loved her too. How was she able to tell?

As summer wore on, Nellie sneaked out a few times to see Andre. I was so scared for her because nothing good would come of this. Her comment was that she loved him, and he loved her. They met any chance they got. Their signal was a screeching nighthawk sound three times, then nothing. Nellie would reply with the same sound, only not as loud, and then she quietly went outside. They would meet at a prearranged place. This went on all summer. I was so worried and scared for her.

One night, Nellie came in after seeing Andre, crying her heart out. She woke Noora, who slept in our room and she started to cry as well. I had a hard time making them both stop. When Noora fell asleep, Nellie and I went outside.

Nellie put her arms around me and wept again. "Andre is leaving to go to work on a big project. They are building big homes in Toronto and are paying men good money to work there. He was going to go there to earn some money, and then he'd come back and get me. We will get married. I will run away and marry Andre!" She loved him more than anything or anyone.

She was so heartbroken. "What am I going to do? Our parents will never let me go. His parents will be very unhappy too, because I am not Ukrainian."

Andre left, and Nellie moped around. Once in a while, one of Andre's brothers would meet with Nellie, to give her a note about how much Andre missed her and loved her.

Two long months went by. Nellie was in a panic because she had not gotten her period. We knew that if she did not get them, she was pregnant. Nellie worried that Papa and Mama would never let her marry out of our Russian heritage. "What shall I do?" she pleaded.

We stayed awake all night, whispered, and planned. This was a scary time for us because we were very immature. We decided in the morning that we would send a message to Andre, through his brothers.

In the morning, Nellie got up early, went to the outhouse, and took water with her to get washed up. After a few minutes she came running to me. Her comment was "We do not have to do anything. I am not pregnant—I am bleeding. I am all right."

They still exchanged notes and stayed in touch through the other brothers.

Over a year went by. One day we saw Andre's brother Nick, and he told us the sad news. They'd buried his brother Andre three days ago. He had fallen off a ladder and broken his back; according to Nick, Andre had not felt any pain, and it happened so quickly. Nick was sorry he could not come and tell Nellie sooner. Nellie was heartbroken, and it was so sad. It was a secret that she and I kept forever.

Time for Marriage

I am sure our parents suspected something was going on. Nellie was old enough to get married. What did they do? They started hinting to her. Mr. and Mrs. Papov came to call from a village near Yorkton. Then before winter was over, they brought their son, Alosha. He was a nice, handsome lad who was short and sort of good looking. We all liked him, much to Nellie's chagrin. He was not Andre and would never be Andre. But both sets of parents agreed that the couple should get married.

After a long winter of weaving, knitting, crocheting, and sewing, Nellie had a hope chest and clothes to wear for the wedding and a long time after. Poor Nellie was unhappy. She did not like Alosha, let alone love him. She begged Papa not to give her away to him, but our parents' minds were made up.

Come spring, she married him with a few prayers and singing from the village people. There was a small meal, and then Nellie was sent on her way to start her married life. It was supposed to be her happy day, but she was anything but happy.

It was lonely without my older sister, but there was still Noora, who was no longer a baby. She was walking, running, and talking, and she got a lot of loving from all of us.

Learning English

In the little settlement of Pelly, there were all sorts of nationalities, so a one-room school went up. According to Doukobour beliefs, we were not allowed to go to school. It had something to do with not believing in the government, not going to war, and all kinds of strange beliefs of the religion.

Oh, how I wanted to go to school. I did learn to read and write Russian from Papa, but this was different. We needed to learn English in order to understand, because we were now in Canada, and they spoke English. In the evenings, I would go to the little house where the teacher lived. I would take her a few eggs, some potatoes, a bit of milk, or other vegetables we had on hand, and I got to be friends with her. Her name was Miss Simmons, and she was a kind and beautiful lady, almost as nice as the lady in Cyprus.

She taught me letters and numbers. She gave me a book to write in and a pencil. Every night I went there, I would return with something new I had learned. I would hide the book and pencil under my dress, so my parents would not find out what I was doing.

I kept this up most of the fall and well into winter.

It got too cold to venture out without everyone asking questions, so Miss Simmons and I put off my tutoring until spring.

Nellie was sending news to us. She was very unhappy, and she was not in the family way, which made Alosha unhappy. He wanted children, and the sooner the better. She was in her twenties, and it was time to be a mother. She had no intension of believing in the crazy stuff that Papavs were starting to believe in; they called themselves the Sons of Freedom. She wanted to come back home. She did not like their beliefs, their nudity, and burning down buildings.

We had built a log house by then and were sort of comfortable. Mama even put up curtains that she had knitted, and they were beautiful and lacy. In the evenings, I would still sneak out to go to school. One evening I was hurrying along the path that I had made after all these trips to school. Out from behind the bush came Vasyl, scaring me out of my wits. He told me he had been watching me and listened at the school window for many nights. He wished he could do the same, because he knew I was learning the English language. He would never tell anyone if I let him come and learn with me.

This school stuff continued, as did meeting Vasyl. As I said before, if I was to marry, it would be him, and I believe he felt the same way about me. We were still young, so all we did was hug and kiss good night—but we had to make sure no one was watching us.

Osiya saw us one night and caught us both by our arms. He frightened us and threatened that he would tell our parents. I was too frightened to go to the school house, and Miss Simmons was very worried about me. She came to call and talk to me in secret, so I told her what Osiya had said. She was sort of afraid of him too, and she did not trust him when she was alone and he was around. She told me his son, Waskya, was learning English too.

Vasyl would come to call, and we would both go to the school under the pretense of visiting Miss Simmons. We did see Waskya there a several times; the poor boy was so shy and afraid we would tell someone that he was there, so we had a talk with him. We would not say anything, and he was not so say a word to anyone about us. Promises were made all around.

Life Was Not Easy

Life went on: gardening, working in the fields in the spring and summer, and hard work in the fall putting away food like potatoes, carrots, and beets to last the winter, which was cold and long. That time was taken up with knitting, weaving, sewing clothes by hand, and embroidering our shawls with colored threads. We would grind our own flour by pounding the grains into powder, and we'd make our own bread. We had a cow, and when she was milking we had milk, skimming cream off the top. When we got enough, we would churn butter in a wooden churn Papa had made during the long winter nights. He also made wooden bowls and spoons for everyone, plus some for relatives and friends. We still had a few chickens, and so we got a few eggs.

We all worked hard. Sometimes I would hoe, cultivate, and rake so much that my hands would blister and bleed.

On Sundays we would gather together in a building to pray and sing songs from Russia.

We heard there was unrest in a few of the villages. People were forming a breakaway group and calling themselves Sons of Freedom. Nellie's husband's family was in the group, and so was her husband, Alosha. She was against the breakaway group, and so Papa and a neighbor took horses and a wagon to the village to see what the problem was. She wanted to come home. What was Papa to do? He did not want her in that terrible group, she was not pregnant, she was not yet insane, and she was not going to undress and rebel like the group. She simply wanted to come home.

She packed her stuff, all her belongings, meager as they were, and came home with Papa and his friend. It was a disgrace to leave a husband in those days.

We were not happy to leave her with that radical group. The night she left, two families burned down their homes as they stood around in the nude and sang psalms. We were so glad to have Nellie out of that situation.

Most of the neighbors came around and wanted to know what was happening. A lot of them had cousins and uncle and aunts in that village and were not happy with them. They were the breakaway radical sect of the Doukobours, and everyone was grouped together.

Every time they did something bad, all Doukobours were blamed. We were ashamed of our radical cousins.

Not Just Sick, but Worse

Winter came and went. Spring was on the way, and planting was soon to be done. I seemed to have developed a cold, running nose, sneezing, and a terrible headache. Cold cloths, warm cloths, breathing in steam from a boiling pot, and other remedies did not seem to help. Mama and Papa decided they would ask the midwife, Natasha Ribkoff, what could be done. She lived in another village, so they would send for her and ask for her advice. She was the only person with any knowledge about illness and how to cure it.

In the morning, after I spent a sleepless night, Vasyl came pounding on the door, which he had never done before. He said, "The police went to Trafeeminkoff place, took Osiya, and arrested him. They put handcuffs on him and took him away."

We later learned Osiya had killed his wife. The police were looking for his son but could not find him. Osiya confessed to killing his wife, but he kept saying he did not kill Waskya. The boy was nowhere to be found. The police said there was so much blood in the woodshed where he'd killed his wife with an axe, and that was where he'd always punished his son too. Where had he hidden the body of his son? All wells and buildings were searched, and all fields were looked at, for new holes. Waskya's body was nowhere to be found. He had vanished.

The relatives had a funeral for the poor wife. Prayers were said and sung, and she was buried in an unmarked grave. We never found out what happened to her son, and it was so sad. No body, no Waskya.

Osiya was taken to a bigger town and tried in court with a Russian interpreter. He never admitted to either his wife's or his son's murder. He was put in a jail, either in Winnipeg or Toronto, never to be heard from again.

Sometimes Things Are Not What They Seem

Vasyl came to see me, and he asked me to marry him. That was a day that I'd looked forward to all these years. Of course, I said yes because I loved him very much. He asked Papa for permission. Papa was a bit reluctant after Nellie's bad marriage, but after a few questions that were embarrassing to Vasyl, Papa agreed. We were engaged, to be married in the fall after the harvest was done.

We were so happy that we could hardly wait. We wanted to be together all the time, but under our parents' watchful eyes, we could not, so we stole an occasional kiss and hug. We were so in love.

Someone told my parents about this midwife, Natasha, who had assorted cures for many illnesses. They said they would tell her to call on us.

First, we had to get Natasha to look at me and fix my stuffed-up nose. She came to our village to tend to the birth of one of the ladies a few doors down, and she came to see me. She looked at me, and I was terrified of her. She was a big, fat, smelly lady. She smelled like herbs and grasses and sweat. She probed my ears and stuck a stick up my nose, made me open my mouth, and nearly made me gag on the stick because it had been in my nose first.

I heard her talking to my parents in a hushed voice. "She has adenoids, and tonsils. Tonsils I cannot cure, but for adenoids, I can burn them out with this strong ointment I have. I will be here for a week, and I will fix her up."

I was so scared and worried. That afternoon I met Vasyl and he said, "Do not worry. Everything will be all right. The midwife is very knowledgeable. She will put this ointment up your nose, the adenoids will go away, and you will be able to breathe better."

How I wished it was that simple, how I wished this was not happening to me. "Why me? What did I do wrong?" I complained. I was so worried.

Nellie hugged me and said, "Do not worry, my dear sister. By morning, all this will be in the past. Look what happened to me. I lay awake and worried many nights, and everything worked out all right. I am here to hold your hand. I am so glad to be with you, to see you through. There will be no pain because the midwife knows how to fix things."

That evening, Natasha came and had chai tea with my parents. She said she would put this ointment up my nostrils and tie a piece of cloth to my nose. That cloth was to stay on all night long. She would give me some laudanum to make me drowsy and relaxed, and she would give me some other herbs. I would sleep until morning.

Natasha boiled up something in a little pot she produced from her not-too-clean-looking bundle of stuff tied in a knot. She had all kinds of smelly things there. Then she told me that I had to go wash up. I was still petrified, and my parents and sister sat there with worried looks on their faces that did not help me stay calm. I washed my face, head, and neck as instructed.

Just before bedtime, the midwife came into my room with a glass of rather bitter stuff to drink and a little jar of yellowish-brown stuff. She said it was sulfuric acid and would burn the adenoids out of my nose by morning. She got a stick with a bit of soft cloth on it, she put on this vile-smelling stuff, and told me to breathe through my mouth. She shoved this smelly ointment into first one nostril and then the other. Then she rolled pieces of cloth that did not look too clean up each nostril. She put them in next, to hold the ointment in. Next, she put a white cloth bandana over my nose. "Do not under any circumstances remove this until the morning," she said.

I got drowsy and was glad to see that smelly lady go. I dropped into the bed I shared with Nellie. I do not know how long I slept, but I woke with a start to excruciating pain to my nose, to my face, to the cleft of my mouth, and even to my eyes. I woke Nellie up with my sobbing, and she in turn woke up my parents. I was ready to tear off the cloth off my face.

Mama said, "No, the midwife said not to touch it." I sobbed because the pain was unbearable. Papa ran to get Natasha, who stayed with her relatives a few doors down the road. Daylight was breaking, and so was my heart. The pain got worse.

Soon—but not soon enough—I heard footsteps and

voices on our doorstep. By then, Nellie, Mama, Grandpa, and Grandma were gathered there and crying with me.

The midwife came in the room carrying a coal-oil lantern. She took off the bandana from my face, and I saw her shocked look. She was filled with fear, and as she bent for a closer look, the fear seemed to mount. Papa looked as she commanded him to hold the lantern, and he also gasped with fear in his eyes. "Her nose is gone!" he exclaimed.

She really did fix me up, but not the way she was supposed to.

The midwife took a closer look. She got a long darning needle from her pack, brought it to my nose— actually, closer to my right eye—and poked something. It felt like my whole lower lid was taken off my face. She made Mama get a basin of water, and then she made me sit up. She pushed my face forward and bathed it. All I saw was blood and two little pieces of the dirty cloth that fell away from what was once my nose. Then there was more blood, and all I felt was pain. I thought it would never end. I screamed with pain, and everyone was crying.

The midwife was scared. "Nothing like this has ever happened to me in all my days as midwife. What am I going to do? Do not tell the police—they will put me in jail. Who will feed my six children? My husband is dead, and there is only me."

Papa said, "What about Mariya? What will we do about her nose? That thing you poked thinking was an infection is her tear duct, I think. Look at her upper lip: it looks like a harelip. She is in great pain. Please, stop her pain. A few hours ago, she was a beautiful young lady. Look at her now."

She went to the stove and boiled up some of her herbs and grasses. They were foul-smelling, but everyone insisted I drink the potion. Anything to kill the pain, or kill me.

Finally, I fell into a restless sleep for the next three days. I remembered very little, just drinking smelly stuff, sleeping, and the pain. The pain was indescribable. I remember Mama and Nellie trying to make me eat. I tried, but it hurt to swallow. My mouth hurt, my lips hurt, half of my upper lip was gone, my top gums hurt, and everything felt like it had been burned. My eye hurt, and most of all, my nose hurt. Nellie said it was gone. How could it hurt if it was gone? How could my pretty, upturned nose be gone?

She told me Vasyl had come to call, and he was very worried about me. All I could do was cry. My parents would not let anyone come to see me.

Finally, Vasyl came and begged to see me and talk to me. I was scared and probably scary to him. When he came as far as the door, he would not come any farther; he did not want to disturb me and wanted me to rest. He said, "Get better."

"Get better how?"

Vasyl ran and told Miss Simmons what he had seen when he came to see me. Miss Simmons came that evening to see me, to speak to me. She wanted to know who'd done this to me. She wanted to know if my parents had done did this to me, and if my relatives were involved. In my best English, I told her what had happened.

She said, "The police have to be told. The midwife has to be stopped. She cannot go on like this, ruining people's lives."

I begged her not to say anything, because the midwife had six children to feed, and they would be orphans if something happened to her. Who would help all the women who had trouble giving birth? The people needed her. I felt so sorry for her children.

Two weeks went by, and then the police came, to talk to me. "Who did this to you? We have to hear it from you. You have to tell us. We know Natasha Ribkoff did this to you, but you have to tell us. You have to charge her with this bad thing she did to you. That way she cannot do this to anyone else. Just tell us she did this."

I suffered so much, but I told the police I could not charge her because she had children to feed, and I did not want to be responsible for the poor orphans' futures. I would suffer even more. I would not say anything officially that would put the midwife in jail.

I felt so sorry for Natasha and her children. How could I charge her? What would I gain if I said anything? I would not get my nose back.

The police were from a bigger city. They went home and told the detachment what was going on. They would keep an eye on the midwife and what she was doing. She could not practice medicine on anyone. She was just a midwife to help during childbirth only.

From a bigger town, the only doctor, Dr. Cromptom, came to see me. He took a look at my nose (or no nose), the torn tear duct, the partial upper lip, and all the flesh burned off by sulfuric acid. He said there was not much he could do, but he had a friend in Brandon, Manitoba, who may be able to help. There was something new in medicine that could help. It was called grafting, where they grew a piece of skin to replace a missing part.

Something had to be done. I had seen a man who burned his finger off, and it was not replaced. What could they do for my nose? How could they regrow my nose? "Oh, Lord, where are you when I need you most?" I prayed.

Help Does Come

In the meantime, the whole town of Yorkton heard about my sad situation. The people of our village started to raise money. What little people had, they gave, as did people in the outskirts of town. Most of our neighbors were very generous. The people in Verigin, Michado, Pelly, and all over the place gathered money.

The kindly Dr. Crompton came often to give me medication to keep me out of pain and see how I was doing. All I did was cry. The torn tear duct would puff up just below my eye, and I would use a handkerchief to squash it gently in order to drain the tears because they were not coming through as normal. There was no nose and no upper lip.

One day Dr. Crompton came, and he was smiling. "My friend in Brandon, Manitoba, said he would look at you and see if there was anything that could be done to fix your nose. He is a very learned man and knows a great deal about surgery, grafting, and medication. I know it will be expensive, but we have gathered a great deal of money to help you to get to Brandon and get started on your treatment."

I was so afraid. I had to leave my family and friends.

I had to leave Vasyl, whom I loved. Was I being fair to tie him down to me and my misery, to my ugly face with no nose and no lips to kiss?

I thought hard. What had I done to deserve this? What was I expected to do? Finally, I decided what I had to do. I had to let Vasyl go. He was nice, and he deserved a better life, a better wife and family. He had to forget me, but I would never forget him. My life was ruined, but he had to live his life without me.

I sent Nellie to tell Vasyl to meet me tonight, in our secret place; he knew where that was. It was a nice night, but I was very sad. I had to be brave and I could not cry. I had to be strong.

I wrapped a kerchief around my face to cover my ugly scars. It was very horrid when I looked in the mirror. My parents wanted to know where I was going. I told them I was breaking off my engagement to Vasyl. They did not say more and were also sad. They knew I was to go away and leave them.

I was very brave, or tried to be. Vasyl put his arms around me, and he could not even kiss me on the lips because I'd tied the kerchief so only my eyes were visible. I did not want anyone, especially Vasyl, to see me like this. I told him I was breaking off the engagement, and that he was to go on without me, start a new life, and find a new wife.

He sobbed and said he would wait for me. He would go to Brandon and get a job to be near me.

I was strong and insisted. "No, you and I cannot wait for each other. I am not happy. I do not want you to be unhappy. Eventually you will grow to hate me. I want you to start a new life without me."

After telling him this, I ran and ran. I hurt all over. My face was sore, but my heart was breaking. "Lord God, where are you? Where are you when I need you?" But no one answered me. I finally went home. There was no light on; my parents did not want to see my hurt look or hear me cry. They did not want me to see them so sad and hurting either. Nellie was awake when I walked into our shared room. She did not say anything but put her arms around me and held me tight. She seemed to understand a bit of what I was going through. I finally went to sleep, and it was a very long night.

The next day, all our friends knew Vasila and I had broken our engagement. Things like that were rarely secret when people lived in close proximity to each other. I would not go outside at all.

The Beginning of a New Life

A few weeks went by, and Dr. Crompton came to call. He told us the arrangements had been made for me to go to Brandon. He handed me an envelope full of money. I had not seen so much money in my whole life. I was to leave in a week, on the train from Yorkton.

In Brandon, Dr. Graham, his wife, and his family would meet the train and take me home with them. I would live with them and do little jobs to help. That way it would not cost me anything for the treatment. He would place me in the hospital when necessary and do the operations. I would live in their house with them.

Miss Simmons came to say good-bye. She brought me a package, a beautiful dress. I'd never worn a dress before, just our traditional Russian blouses and skirts made of spun wool. My mother made me a nice green outfit. The teacher told me to take the dress with me and wear it in Brandon. There were no traditional clothes there, and she did not want me to feel out of place. She was so thoughtful, and I thanked her for teaching me the English language, for the dress, and for being so nice to me. I missed her already.

My cousin brought me some pretty underclothing to

wear, and another cousin crocheted me a dainty kerchief to wear on my trip.

Papa managed to get me beautiful shoes to wear. Nellie gave me her beautiful cotton flowered blouse; she'd made it smaller to fit me. All the friends and neighbors were so nice and generous. A lot were nosy and curious. They came to see what I looked like. I would not remove the cover from my face for any one.

Then the gossips came, saying that Vasyl was seen talking to one of the girls a few doors down, though they would not tell me who it was.

Of course I hurt, and I cried because I missed him. But I did the right thing by telling him to find someone else. Regardless of whom he saw, I hoped he would be happy.

Two days before I left, Vasyl came to see me. He wanted me to change my mind about us, but I said. He then told me his parents and my friend Paula's parents wanted them to get together. He was not in favor of their matchmaking. I was jealous but wished him the best of luck and happiness in his future. I gave him a final hug and said good-bye. Then I went away and secretly cried. I could not even cry properly; the duct below my right eye bulged and hurt, and I had to push on it to drain it. I felt so forsaken. It was not Vasyl's fault, but my own. I knew it was not really my fault either.

Then came the day to leave our little village of Pelly. Papa borrowed a wagon from a neighbor, and Mama and Nellie and I got in it. All my friends and relatives, as well as nosy neighbors, came to see us off. Vasyl was in the back bunch, and he called out well wishes. Some cried, and all waved and said good-bye. We went on our way to Yorkton. I sobbed.

I had a little bag of clothes. Papa made a comb from a cow horn, and Mama made some soap. I had Miss Simmons's dress and all the new underthings my cousins had given me. It should have been an adventure I dreamed about, but I left with a heavy heart. I did not realize how bad I had felt until we were on the way. It was a long ride, and last time I'd walked it, but now it felt longer.

In Yorkton we stayed at Mama's cousin's house. We slept on the floor on blankets. I tried to sleep, but all I could do was cry. Doing so silently was impossible. I tried to tell myself that it was going to be all right, but it was not all right. I could not sleep.

Journey to Brandon

The train was in the station when we arrived. Papa got me the ticket, gave it to me, and held me in his arms like it was going to be the last time. Mama and Nellie hugged me tightly and kissed me good-bye, like I was leaving and never coming back. When the whistle blew, I reluctantly got on the train with my meager package of belongings clutched tightly by my side. This was all I had; I did not even have my parents or sisters anymore. I did not have Vasyl, and I did not have a life. All I had was fear. "Oh, God. What is to become of me?"

I got a window seat and pulled my shawl over my face so that all one could see was my eyes. I glanced out the window, and there stood Papa, Mama, and Nellie, looking sad. For their sake, I tried to sit up straighter and appear brave. As the train pulled out of the station, we waved at each other, trying not to cry. I waved until I could not see them. Then I sobbed behind my shawl, into the cold glass of the window of the train.

Soon I felt a kindly tap on my shoulder. It was a man dressed in a nice suit. He said he wanted my ticket. I realized it was the conductor and he was collecting tickets. He was very kind looking, and he smiled at me.

Two seats down, in front and opposite me, was a younger mother and her child. The little girl was curious about me and kept staring at me. Finally, I heard her say very loudly to her mother, "Mommy, she has no nose!"

"Hush," her mother replied.

But the little girl kept looking at me and whispering to her mother.

I turned to the window and looked out at the passing scenery. All was flat, with not too much to see. I must have dozed off, because the train whistle blew loudly, and I woke with a start. The present world came crashing back around me. I felt so sorry for myself. I was in such a sad situation—scared to be on my own, scared of the world around me, and scared of the future. I was worried about my parents, about my sister, and about what people thought of my horrible nose. I even worried about Natasha the midwife, who had done this to my face. I worried about her children and hoped nothing would happen to them. All my worrying did not help.

The conductor of the train came through and asked me if I wanted anything to eat. I did not, because I had bread my mother had insisted I take with me. I was simply thirsty. He came around with water and gave me a glass. It was so refreshing, and I gulped it down.

We made a few stops at small villages. People got on and off the train. It seemed that everyone who went past my seat stared at me. It was then and there I made up my mind that I was going to be this way all my life, and I had to get used to all the stares, the shocked and disgusted looks, and the "I feel sorry for you" looks. *From this day forward, I am not going to let it bother me, or I will tolerate it.*

Finally darkness came, and the train coach quieted down. I think I slept. When I awoke, I took my belongings, went to the back where the toilets were, and relieved myself. There was a basin with running water, and I washed up the best I could while trying not to look in the mirror. I went back to my seat and tried not to look in the window at my reflection.

It was a long journey to Brandon, Manitoba. The conductor finally announced that we were approaching Brandon, and people hustled around, getting their belongings together. Women were pulling out mirrors and checking their faces. A mirror—that was something I did not have, because I did not want to see my face. I clutched my meager belongs in my lap and looked out the window. We soon pulled into the station, and people were milling around. I wondered if anyone was there to meet me. I did not have to worry as I stepped from the train.

My New Home

There was a kind-looking gentleman, and beside him stood his wife with a big smile for me. Beside her was a young lad, their son.

Dr. Graham, introduced himself. "This is my wife, Gretchen, and our son, Ernest. We call him Ern, and you can too. You, of course, are Mary. Can we call you Mary, or do you have a different name?"

"No," I said as I shook my head, embarrassed. "Mary is all right."

Mankiya or Mariya was unpronounceable and sort of childish in my new world. Yes, my new world, my new life, my new family. They all sounded so friendly, so kind. I could not stop the tears that slid down my cheeks.

Dr. Graham took the bag from me and walked ahead. His wife followed, waving me on, and then she held my nervous hand. Ern brought up the rear. We all got into a nice black car. I had seen cars but had never been in one.

Ern and I were in the back seat. He had not spoken but glanced at me occasionally. I moved as far as I could against the door, looking out the window. I felt a tear run down my cheek and brushed it away. Soon another came. I had no intention to cry, but I could not help it. I reached into my pocket for a handkerchief, could not find one, and then felt a light touch on my arm. I looked down to see a neatly folded men's handkerchief with the letter "E" embroidered on it. I tried to shake my head no, but Ern pushed it toward me, so I took it and wiped away my tears.

We drove for a while and then pulled into a driveway in front of a large white house with a green roof. Never in my life had I seen a green roof, let alone such a beautiful house with a green door, green shutters, and green trim. The white looked so clean and shiny.

Dr. Graham jumped out, opened Gretchen's door, and then opened mine. "Here we are. This is going to be your home from now on," he said while smiling broadly.

Ern took my bag and ran ahead of us. He opened the green door, and out bound a friendly, furry creature barking and wagging his tail. Ern said, "This is Mary. Mary, meet Badger." The dog was so excited that he came and rubbed against me, nearly pushing me over. He stopped and licked my hand. I guessed we would be friends from then on.

We entered into a large hall. I could see into the living room, with large couches and chairs. The dining room had a large, beautiful table set with gold-trimmed china, crystal glasses, and glistening silverware—all a novelty to me.

Gretchen motioned for me to follow her, up the curved staircase. Upstairs, I was led to a bedroom that had a closet to hang the few clothes I had. There was also a dresser, a large mirror, and another door that opened to something I had never envisioned. There was a cupboard with a basin built into it, as well as taps one turned to get water. Beside that was a toilet like on the train. Gretchen showed me how, if I pulled this chain, water would run into it and flush everything away. She told me to wash my face. In the cupboard were fresh, nice-smelling, pink towels. She motioned they were for me to use, and then turned me around and showed me a large bathtub and how to turn on the water. There was hot and cold water. All this was for me to use! This was new to me. It was like a private house just for me.

She left me to survey my new home. As I stood in the middle of the room, there was a soft knock on the door. Ern brought my meager parcel with my belongings. I said thanks, and he left. I could not believe all the new things. If my situation were any different, I probably would have enjoyed my surroundings more.

The door opened a crack. I looked up and could not see any one. I should have looked down, because there came the cutest ball of fluff like it belonged here. It raised its cute little head and meowed. I picked it up, and it started to purr. I knew I had a friend for life. As I cried, it purred louder, making me cry more.

I heard a tap on the door. It was Ern, and he told me dinner was ready, so I should wash my face and come downstairs. It took me a few minutes to compose myself. Finally I went down the stairs of this beautiful house. Everyone was waiting for me.

The kindly doctor pulled out a chair and motioned for me to sit down. When everyone was seated, a lady dressed in a nice navy dress and white apron brought in food. First was soup. Mine was different from the others; Gretchen told me it was all vegetables, and the rest of my meal was vegetarian, because the doctor from Yorkton had informed them that I did not eat meat. I did have eggs, vegetables, cheese, and nuts. I had plenty to eat. Dessert was apple pie, and it was delicious with ice cream on top. It was the best meal I'd ever had.

After dinner, I strolled into the kitchen and offered to help wash the dishes. There was another lady there, with the one who'd served us, and they would not hear of it; it was their job. They had kindly smiles for me.

I walked outside, and Badger was very happy to see me. I sat and petted him. It was getting cooler outside, so I went in. Gretchen called me into the living room, and there was soft music coming from what was called a radio—how interesting. She then informed me that tomorrow a special teacher was coming to tutor Ern, and she would also teach me while I lived there. It was getting late, so Gretchen went upstairs with me and showed me how to fill the tub. She told me I could bathe every day— or more if I desired.

She said good night. Then she looked toward my bed and said, "Fluffy, what are you doing in Mary's bed? Mary, I hope you do not mind our pets."

"I love them!" I replied. Fluffy was curled up in a little ball at the foot of my bed, and so Gretchen left him there.

I had a long bath and washed my hair; all my curls were still there. I left the door ajar a bit for Fluffy to get out. When I finally hit the pillow, I was out like a light.

Before I knew it, morning was here. I closed the door and did my morning washing, I was afraid to use the toilet, but I had to. When I pulled the chain as previously instructed, there was a gush of water, and all was clean. Everything was so new to me.

Even breakfast was exciting: eggs, toasted bread with jam, and coffee with milk and sugar.

After breakfast, it was school time for Ern and me. Ern was so smart because he could read and write, and Miss Pearce told me I soon would be able to do all that. She gave me a book, pencils, and a scribbler to write on. First it was my name, and she printed it on a blackboard. I was to do the same on my scribbler, which I neatly did. Then she wrote it. It was harder to do, but I did it. Before I knew it, I did the alphabet and numbers. She taught me some syllables and short sentences. I was so excited, and I even wrote Badger's and Fluffy's names. We did two hours of school work in the morning and then three hours in the afternoon. I think Ern was glad to have company. Before I knew it, the day was gone.

The following week, I had no school. I went with Dr. Graham to the place they called the hospital. There were other doctors there and many nurses. Everyone looked at my nose and face. At first I was scared and embarrassed, but they were polite and very gentle.

They were speaking so quickly that I did not understand everything that was happening. I was given a special gown to wear, and it had ties on the back. Doctors listened to my heart (which I was sure was pounding) and to my lungs. They looked at my hands, especially my left thumb. What did that have to do with my nose? They checked my reflexes, looked at my upper arm, and bent it toward my face. They were nodding and saying, "It will work out all right."

That night I hardly slept at all. I worried and cried. I agreed to do whatever the doctors decided had to be done. They knew best.

The next day, I went back to the hospital. The doctors were there again, and Dr. Graham explained to me that they would build me a new nose, but I would have to give up my left thumb for it. They would fix my upper lip. I did not completely understand. I nodded my head to go ahead with whatever they decided. I signed a lot of papers that I did not understand. It was a good thing I had learned to write my name.

I understood that nothing could be done with the torn tear duct; it would fill up, and I would have to press down on it to get the tears out. I would have to live with that. The nose was measured, and my left thumb was measured and remeasured by being put up to my nose many times. My upper arm was also put up to my nose, and they asked if I could hold it there for a long time.

In days to come, I realized when they said a long time they meant weeks or a month, not just days.

Dr. Graham said, "We will begin your surgery the next day. Now, you go home and have the rest of the day off. Ern will take the afternoon off and show you around Brandon. Maybe you can go out and have some ice cream."

I walked slowly to the doctor's house. That was now my home. I offered to help, but Mrs. Graham would not even hear of it, so I went upstairs and had my usual cry.

Soon Ern came along and told me to put on my shoes, a warm sweater, and the usual kerchief. It was getting cool outside and looked like rain. I did as I was told. We went outside and walked toward the center of town. I loved looking into the store windows and seeing all the interesting, beautiful things. There were things I had never seen or even imagined. Everything was new to me. We stopped for a soda, and it was heaven, poured in a fancy glass.

Then we continued walking past the theater. Ern said some day he would take me to a movie, and he tried to explain a picture show. It sounded strange to me.

We continued to the hospital grounds, and he showed me where I would stay for my operation. I listened very carefully, trying to understand every word he told me. Then we continued around the backside of the building. I was told this was a residence for the mentally ill, for people who had problems dealing with everyday things and needed help coping with daily needs such as meals and washing. It was so hard to comprehend all these things.

Ern said, "Come. I will show you. They will be getting a small snack this time of the day. Maybe we can help. I have done this many times. Etta, the nurse and helper here, lets me help sometimes."

We went in the back entrance. Sure enough, there was a cart with juice and cookies loaded up at one of the doors, ready to be served to the patients, as the sick ones were called. Etta was there. She told us we could go in with her. She cautioned that we had to stay close to her, be quick, and close and lock the doors behind us as we passed through.

At the first door, she unlocked it and pushed the cart through. We went in quickly behind her, and she locked the door right after us. That was when I heard a noise like I had never heard before. It was a combination of swearing, wailing, and screeching. Oh, what a scary sound.

We headed to the next door, and we were close behind Etta. Everyone grabbed at the food and the juice-filled glasses. They grabbed at Ern, Ette, and me. One of the big men grabbed at Etta's key to the doors before she had a chance to close the second door, never mind lock it. All the patients rushed and pushed out of the first entrance door. Everyone screamed—including us.

One of the nurses in the main part of the hospital ran screaming for the staff to come quickly. Soon there were doctors, nurses, and police all over the place. Some of the patients got out of the main building and ran down the street.

I do not believe I'd been so frightened in my whole life. I shook so hard that I could hardly stand. We were outside the hospital so quickly. Ern and I ran home as fast as we could. That evening at the supper table, we got a lecture about being careful and going places we should not go. It was an excellent lesson learned the hard way.

Most of the patients were quickly found and returned to the hospital. One of the patients was found thirty miles away four days later, frightened and hungry, hiding in a hay shed on a farm.

Operation Number One

Come the morning, it was the day for my thumb to come off, or so I thought. I was wrong: this was the day for the skin on my thumb to be removed and then reunited with my so-called nose. I was so groggy that I could not think straight. I was told I would be on medication to relax me and make me drowsy. Mrs. Graham and Ern came to see me, and they both held my free hand; the other one was busy getting grafted to my nose and upper lip. My whole arm was held immobile. I was so dopey that I was sure they did not understand what I was saying.

There were doctors and nurses around, trying to keep me comfortable. I tried to put my left arm down but could not. The nurses told me I was to leave it right where it was taped and secured to my face. My food was served through a straw, mostly milky or fruity drinks. When I had to go to the bathroom, I would have a flat potty slipped under me. It was degrading, but I had to do what had to be done. After a few days, it did not matter, and I slept most of the time.

When I was awake and out of pain, I would look around me. One day there was an Armenian lady in the bed next to me. She spoke and understood some Russian, and she spoke very kindly to me and tried to console me, to make me stop crying.

There were different patients with different ailments in the bed next to mine, and they came and went. I stayed, sleepy and groggy.

A little girl, five years old, was brought into the bed beside me one day. She could not walk; her legs were crooked and looked like they were soft. She was lacking calcium, I was told. I watched the nurse crush eggshells into a fine powder and mix this powder with finely beaten eggs, milk, cocoa, and sugar; sometimes she'd add fruit like raspberries and strawberries. Then other nurses would come to exercise her legs a several times a day.

I do not remember how much time passed, but before one knew it, the little girl's legs were stronger. Soon she was able to stand and take a few steps. After a few weeks, she was able to walk. I walked with her, when I was allowed to get up out of bed. Six weeks seemed like an eternity, but the little girl was released from the hospital.

Then it was my day to get operated on, and my thumb had to be cut off and become part of my nose. Doctors said my lip would be all right. I was wheeled into the operating room, and one of the doctors stuck a needle into my right arm. All I could remember was the bright lights on the ceiling.

I was in my room when I awoke. The first thing I did was look at my left hand and my thumb—or should I say, no thumb. All I saw was a white bandage up to the elbow. *Did they take off the entire hand?* I started to cry. The nurse came and made me drink something. I do not remember much, except I wondered that if my thumb was grown to my nose, why couldn't I feel it? And why was my left thumb sore if it was not there? I carefully reached up to my nose and lip, but all I felt were more bandages. How scary. I was worried about the unknown.

I was bandaged up and kept out of pain for days. It seemed like an eternity, and I was groggy most of the time. I remember Mrs. Graham coming to see me, and I think Ern was there sometimes. I ate, slept, and worried. Mostly, I worried.

One day, a relative of Mama's came to see me. She was married to a cousin of Mama, and her name was Loosha. She told me everything was all right with my parents and the girls. Nellie was very pleased to be home, and Noora was becoming a beautiful girl. Oh, how I missed everyone. It seemed like such a long time since I'd seen them. She told me Vasyl had married Polly, one of my friends from Pelly. I wished them well.

Though I was all bandaged up, I asked her questions about my condition, which she was unable to answer. Loosha also told me there was talk about the Doukobours moving to British Columbia, a mountainous territory of Canada four hundred miles from the west coast. As a matter of fact, a few small groups had left in 1908, to get things established. I was surprised because I'd never heard of this. It was like I was in another world, even as we were speaking of it. She filled me in on some of the meetings they had in our village, and it was put to a vote. Those who wanted to stay in Saskatchewan would be allotted farmland that they could run, or they could go to British Columbia and live in communes, as they had done all their lives. Most of my relatives agreed to go, as had my parents and grandparents.

Would they go and leave me here, so far away?

My aunt Dasha, who had married Soma Nadane, had moved into Kamsack and opened up a retail food and clothing store. Soma's parents lived on a farm of their own for a while, so they helped them to get things going on the new venture. I was so happy for her.

A great deal of people got land in Saskatchewan and stayed.

I was worried. "Will I ever see my family again?"

Loosha assured me that things would work out, and when I got well, I would find a way to be reunited with them.

After much hugging and crying, Loosha left with my best regards to all my friends and relatives when she saw them. I asked her to tell them I was going to be all right.

Then came the day when the bandage came off my thumb. Dr. Graham and his colleagues said it had healed beautifully. The stub I had for a thumb was beautiful. It was cut off at the second joint, and there was a bit of a scab in the middle where the rest of the thumb had been. My thumb hurt, but how could a thumb hurt when it was not there? The doctor told me it was the nerve endings that hurt, but they would heal and not hurt anymore. I did not understand.

For my nose, I sat up while they slowly removed the bandages. The doctors and nurses were curious, and all I could see were faces looking down at me. I was very scared, but there were no horrified or disgusted looks, just curiosity. With a lot of probing and nodding of heads, I was finally handed a mirror. A scared and worried face looked back at me—a face with a blood-red protuberance where a nose should have been. The lip did not look too bad; the missing gap was filled with a bright red scar. I started to weep. The doctors assured me that this could be fixed. They showed me my upper arm, where they would take the skin and grow it, to the nose. They would build me a proper nose.

I had a choice to wait for a few weeks or go ahead with the rest of the procedure, or getting the skin grafted. I let the doctors decide. The doctors figured I needed a break and a rest.

After a break, the time for surgery came again. I was kept sedated for days and fed liquids through a straw. I slept most of the time, my left arm over my face secured with soft bandages. When I was awake, I was told not to move. This was similar to the procedures I'd gone through with the thumb. I tried not to think and worry about myself.

Mrs. Graham came to see me often, brought me books to read, and helped me with my studies.

Soon, another six weeks had gone by, and it was time for the skin to be removed from my upper arm. The graft had taken very well, according to the doctors. Once again I was knocked out, and I woke up with pain in my upper arm. What a relief to be able to put my left arm down and move it around! The arm was bandaged up, and so was my nose. The nurses would change the bandage on my face every day, but they would not give me a mirror to look. I was again worried—not that I ever fully stopped worrying.

I was able to get up and move around, as well as go to the bathroom myself—no bedpan what a relief! I could get in the bathtub and have a bath instead of a wet cloth bath.

I never realized all the things one appreciated until one had them taken away. I tried not to feel sorry for myself, but it was hard to do.

Ern came and helped me with my schoolwork, and he had me reading out loud. He would only correct me when I made a mistake or mispronounced a word. He was so patient, and I was willing to learn everything I could.

Pretty soon I was able to go home to the doctor's house and to my own bedroom. I returned to Badger and Fluffy, who was no longer a kitten, though he was still beautiful. He still loved me and slept at the foot of my bed.

I continued to take my schooling and learned more and more. I still had to go to the hospital to get rebandaged and make sure there was no infection. The nose was there, but it was an ugly little knob with two nostrils below it. The lip was sort of okay, or at least it did not look like a harelip any more. The red soon disappeared, but the tear duct would have to stay the way it was. When it filled up, I would use a clean handkerchief to press down on it. The doctors decided to do another operation and fix things up a little better. This was to take place in a month or so.

In the meantime, it was summer. There were to be summer holidays with no lessons, because the teacher was taking off the summer. Mrs. and Dr. Graham found little jobs for me to do, like ironing the doctor's shirts and a few blouses for Gretchen. They said they would pay me, but how would I repay them for my lovely place to stay and the food they gave me?

One day a Ukranian lady came over and conversed with me in her language. It was very similar to Russian, so I understood her quite well. She wanted me to go shopping with her, because I could speak English and she could not. I would be very helpful to her and some of her friends who did not speak the language. She said they would pay me for these services. This was all right with the doctor and his family; I would still have my room and my meals with them.

I would have a job and earn my own money. That would be one way I could save money for my trip to my parents in British Columbia, when they moved there. I did get a letter from Nellie, and she told me about the move.

I went to the hospital once more and saw the same nurses who had treated me the previous times. They were happy to see me. I was not happy to be there, even if it was nice to see them.

I was put under once more, and the doctors tried to fix the nostrils and make them more normal. One showed great improvement, but the other was sort of distorted and stuck under my nose. At least it was better than it had been; after all my nose had been through, this was better than I had expected.

The doctors and nurses were so good to me. This time, I was in the hospital three weeks before the bandages came off. The doctors said I did not need to wear them anymore. I still had an infection and had to clean the nose and nostril area twice a day; the nurses taught me how to do this. If it ever got infected, again, I was to use a yellow powder dissolved with warm water, and clean gauze. I was too embarrassed not to wear the bandage. I was embarrassed when someone looked at me with a stare or curious look. I did not go out in public without the bandage over my nose. I keep gauze over the nose area and under the eyes, and I tied it up under my hair, at the back of my head.

The doctors were trying to encourage me to go without the bandage, but I was too self-conscious when out in public. This way, people could not see my nose and ask questions. The nurses and doctors gave up.

I had to see Dr. Graham and his team of doctors every month. I lived with the good doctor and his family, and I studied with Ern. They were my extended family, and I loved them dearly.

Ern was going to be a doctor like his father, and he studied hard. He went to high school and then on to university. When he was home, which was for most holidays, he found time to spend with me and to see I got my schooling. His mother missed him and was very happy to have me around, and she saw to it that I did my studying. She took me shopping and made sure I had nice clothes to wear. Ern got a scholarship go McGill University. I missed him; he was the brother I'd never had.

At Christmastime, gifts were exchanged. With me working, I managed to get little gifts for everyone, including the dog and cat. We put them under the tree, which was a novelty to me, but I started enjoying that tradition every year.

I went on shopping trips with Irena and her friends. I

went to dentists, went to doctors, and headed everywhere they needed an interpreter.

Irena and I once went to a hairdresser, Golden Hair Salon. She was getting her hair cut and curled. She convinced me to cut my hair. When the hairdresser washed my hair, she combed it up and out. I ended up with the nicest curls all over my head. I did not realize my hair was so curly; it looked so nice. No longer would I braid my hair and put it in a bun.

One day Irena went into a dress shop, and I saw something in the window that caught my eye. All of a sudden, someone grabbed my sleeve and turned me around. There stood a tall, good-looking, tanned man.

"Mankiya, whatever happened to you?" said Waskya Trafeeminkoff.

Oh, dear—a voice from the past! I explained how everyone had looked for him. I briefly explained what had happened to me and why I was in Brandon. Most of all, I said how happy I was to see that he was alive.

He told me that he had had to run away. He was afraid of his father because he had seen him kill his mother. He read in the newspapers that his father was in prison for life, and that they could not find him. He never wanted to see his father again, because the man had abused him since he was a baby. There was nothing to be gained by telling anyone he was all right because he had no relatives or anyone who cared about him. He said he had a job and worked hard, was well liked at work, and had a small place in which to live. Lately he'd been seeing a very nice girl, but he would never tell her or anyone about his past.

He told me his name now was Wallace Grey. He said

he had to talk to me, because he recognized me, and our family had always been nice to him and his mother. He felt sorry for me and wished me the best. He made me promise not to tell anyone that I'd seen him. With a quick hug, he ran off down the street.

It was like a dream. I turned and went into the shop. Irena had not even missed me. I stood by the window and looked out. No, it was not a dream. I saw Waskya—or I should say Wallace—throw a package into the back of a truck, hop in, and drive away. It was him, all right. He was very much alive! I felt so sorry for him, yet I was very happy for him.

I saved my money. I had a little can with a lid in the dark corner of my clothes closet, and every once in a while, I would take it out and count it. I had more money than I'd ever dreamed of having. Sometimes I would count the coins, and Fluffy would bat them around with his paws.

One day I went shopping with Irena's friend Luba. She needed shoes, and we went to a store that had a sale. She picked out a pair of shoes that were a size too big for her feet, but she insisted that the price was right and it was more leather for the bigger size. When she went to pay for the shoes they were two pairs for the same price, so she insisted that she would get a pair for me; that was to be my payment for going shopping with her. I got shiny patent-leather shoes with heels that made me look a few inches taller. How proud I was, and I had earned them myself!

Soon It Was Over

That was how I spent the next three years of my life: the hospital and lots of doctor visits. I helped the Grahams with the flower gardens, ironed clothes to pay for my lodging, did my translating for the Ukrainian ladies, and learned the English language.

In between all this, Ern took me to my first movie show. He borrowed a bicycle from a friend and taught me how to ride it. His friends accepted me as one of them, and the bandaged nose did not matter to them. I was their friend, and I was one of them. They took me dancing one evening, and all of Ern's friends took turns dancing with me.

I had friends of my own too. The girls put makeup on me, and I wore lipstick for the first time. My parents and grandparents would be horrified if they ever found out. I enjoyed doing everything I had never done before, and I did things I should not have been doing. However, I felt that if I was not hurting myself or anyone else, how could I be doing wrong? For once in my life, I enjoyed myself.

Irena and I discussed this one afternoon. She laughed at some of my family's beliefs and thinking. She told me to get on with my life because I would never go back to the past. She herself would not want to go back to the past, even if there was a way to do it. She said the whole world was changing every day, and we had to live in it and change with it.

I had to remember this. I would not get my nose back. I would not get my old boyfriend back. And would I really want him back after he had been with another woman? The answer was no.

"Just remember, every day is a new beginning. Every day, something new can happen. Whatever happened yesterday is never to be again, and tomorrow is another beginning of something new," said Irena.

That was the day I decided I would live every day as it came. However things were handed to me, I would handle them at the time and try not to worry about them until they happened. It was a hard thing to do, but I tried.

One day I was out with Irena to get her eyes checked; she needed glasses to read. That was when I found out that I could not read the chart either. Dr. Kress did Irena's eye test, and Irena was asking questions as I was translating. Then the optometrist asked me if I'd ever had my eyes tested. When I said no, he told me to come back the next day and do some ironing for his wife, and he would check my eyes.

That was how I got the glasses that I needed badly. How much better I could see! I could easily read books and realized how much I had been missing. I did ironing for three weeks for Dr. Kress's wife, to pay for my new glasses. It was worth it.

I went shopping to different places with Irena and learned where I could buy my undergarments at a good price, when the sales were on. I learned what was good quality, what would not wash well, and what was a great buy.

One day one of Irena's friends, Fesha, wanted me to go to the drugstore with her. She told me she needed some bark, to enable her to abort the new baby she was carrying. Her husband was not to know anything about this. They could not afford another child because they had seven already. I had never heard of this, and I was shocked that she could and would do this. She told me it was out there, and all we needed was the right drug store. Her midwife told her what to get and how to use it.

The mention of a midwife frightened me. She told me it was her only hope, so I went with her. I told her what the midwife did to me, but she assured me she had a good one; the woman had delivered her babies, and all was okay. Besides, she would do this procedure herself. She was so sure that it was the right thing to do. All I had to do was talk to the druggist and ask for this stuff, because she did not know enough English to do it herself.

As we were walking past a store window, I spotted a tin-covered travel trunk, and I hesitated to look at it. It was all I needed to take my belonging to British Columbia, and I could buy a few things for my relatives and have them packed in there, to take on the train. Fesha told me if this remedy worked, she would personally buy this for me; it would be cheaper than raising another child.

We found a drugstore that sold the bark. The druggist looked at her and then at me, but he took her money, and we were soon gone. Fesha told me she would get ahold of me later.

Two weeks went by, and then she and her husband pulled up to the Graham house in a nice truck. In the back was the trunk I had admired. Her husband told me he had got a new job that paid twice as much as his old one, and she'd told him she owed me money. This trunk was the payment, and they thanked me for everything. They and their seven children were moving to his new job in Winnipeg. I wished them the best and said thanks.

I could not look at the trunk without thinking of Fesha and her husband, but I would have bought the trunk out of my savings.

I managed to get undergarments for my sisters, shawls for Mama and Grandma, some carving tools for Papa, and a new sweater for Grandpa (something he would never dream of buying for himself). I bought some nice material for new clothes and a few things like pins for the head kerchiefs. I got nice-smelling soaps and some cold cream to put on our faces; these would have to be kept hidden from the grandparents, and the people in our community were not to know. Some things simply were not allowed.

News from Home

In the meantime, my parents and relatives moved to Brilliant, British Columbia. They went on the train and then walked three miles to their little piece of property, in a place called Ootishenia. It was on the Columbia River, just on Waterloo Eddy.

Nellie wrote to me and told me they had nice neighbors, the Swansons, who had two pretty daughters. She talked a bit of English with them. She told me there was a ferry that went across the river to Kinnaird. They lived in Waterloo Landing, but the whole area was called Ootishenia. The area was once populated by miners and loggers and their families, but they all had moved away; some buildings were still there. There was a family by the name of Landis, and they had three boys.

She said there was a large river, the biggest she had ever seen, called the Columbia River. The community was building a bridge across the Kootenay River, which was a large river but not as big as the Columbia. It sounded very interesting to me.

Papa cut logs and built a small house, and he was adding more living quarters for Grandpa and Grandma. Noora and I had a nice bedroom that we shared; it was on the second story of the little place. She wanted to know when I was going to be well enough to travel to the new home.

I told everyone it was going to be soon, but I was afraid of what people would say. What would they think? What would they whisper behind my back? What would they say to me, or to my family? People could be so unkind and say such hurting words, and they could give even more hurting looks.

At that time, I wished I was dead. It would have been easier on everyone, especially me. Where was my resolution? Where was my promise to myself not to worry, not to do things until the time came to be? But I still worried.

Would anyone miss me if I was not around? Would anyone care if I disappeared? Would it matter if I did not awake the next day? All these thoughts and more went through my mind when I lay awake at night or was alone. These were serious matters that only I could answer myself. It was a series of difficult questions, and the answers were even more difficult.

In my mind, I created a poem.

> Oh, woe is me.
> How can these terrible things come to be?
> Cry if I may,
> Will all these terrible things improve someday?
> All the nice people out here
> Cannot remove the sorrow I can share—
> Or do they even care?
> Out of curiosity, so many stare.
> Some show their pity and care.

Some people just glance.
Many look away and hope they do not run into
me by chance.
Oh, woe is me.
How sad can this world be?

I put this little poem to music and would sing it under my breath, when I was sad and alone. I had a good singing voice, and when I was not embarrassed, I could carry a good tune.

One cold, rainy day, Dr. Graham said the doctors wanted to see me in the hospital. They made me put on the backless gown, and they checked my heart, lungs, reflexes, and most of my joints. They checked my back, my neck, the scars on my upper arm, and my thumbless left hand. Then they took the bandages off my nose and told me I did not need these anymore. The doctors told me they were sorry. They had done all that could be done. The tear duct would need to be pressed with clean handkerchiefs to drain.

They presented me with a nicely wrapped package and told me to open it. I carefully opened the package, saving the wrapping. There were twelve beautifully embroidered handkerchiefs, all white and beautifully folded, with different colored flowers on them. They were beautiful, and that was not all. There was an envelope, and they were anxious for me to open it. Inside was a card with many signatures, as well as a train ticket to Brilliant, British Columbia. All the Brandon Hospital staff had started a collection for me to go home.

I was to go home. I'd not dreamed I would be going

home. A new home, and a new beginning. How was I going to handle all this?

I was weeping, and the doctors and the nurses were crying and trying not to show it. In my entire life, I have not had so many hugs and kisses. Everyone was kind to me.

Everything was all right, except I insisted I keep on my bandages. I did not want to face the world with the nose I had. The staff understood, and I received a big bag of bandages and ointment, in case of infection.

I went home with Dr. Graham to prepare for my trip home. I would miss Fluffy the cat and Badger the dog. I would miss the ladies in the kitchen and the cleaning lady, as well as the bathroom I took for granted. Ern was at university, but I would miss him; he was like a brother, and all his friends had become my friends. I would miss Gretchen, who helped me so much, and all the doctors and nurses. I would even miss the hospital. There was also Irena. I would miss her and all the people to whom she'd introduced me. I would miss going shopping and heading to dentists and doctors with them.

I thanked God on my knees that night, for everything, everyone, and all the memories. I thanked God for all he had given me in the last four years, and for all the good things he provided. There were good people in this world.

The next day, I ran all over town to tell everyone the news. All the good people wished me well. Later in the day, some brought little gifts, and others gave me money in an envelope. They were happy for me, and some cried and told me they would miss me.

I packed my neat, tin-covered trunk and then sat and looked at it. It was almost full. I could lift and move one end, then the other. Certainly I could not lift it. How was I going to get it on the train?

Gretchen came in and told me not to worry; I would get help with it, and someone would put it on the train. Staff would transfer it to the next train and take it off at my destination. What a relief. I worried an awful lot.

It Was Time to Go

It was time for another chapter in my life. On the morning I was to leave, I wept at everything and with everyone at the house, then again at the railway station. Irena and my other friends came to say good-bye. It was so sad to leave everyone.

The conductor called, "All aboard."

I sat by a window and waved good-bye to everyone. As I waved, I noticed Waskya, or Wallace, waving with everyone. I wished him the best. I was off to another episode of my life, with the chugging of the train, the ding of the bell, and the sad hoot of the whistle. My heart was in my throat.

I was so scared. *What will I encounter next?* I'd had so many scary things happen, did it really matter?

I sat by the window and looked outside at the prairie, which was flat and uninteresting. I saw an odd clump of trees and a house with other buildings around it. I imagined what it would be like to live there with a husband and children. I threw it all that out of my mind. I would never marry or have any children. Never would any man love me, with a scarred lip, no nose, and no thumb.

I sat with my thoughts. *I will live with myself, by myself.*

I will not let having a disfigured face bother me. If anyone else stares at me, I will pretend to not notice it. If they point and make remarks, I will ignore them.

I realized how hard it was at the next rail station, when a woman with two children got on. There was an available seat across from me, so she sat down with the younger child; her older one sat beside me. I glanced over to find the eight-year-old boy staring at my bandages. Then he got up and whispered to his mother, and all I caught was "Bandit." The mother shook her head, and I turned away again, pretending not to notice.

Then the mother said loudly, "You do not have to sit beside that lady with all that stuff on her face."

Pretty soon the little boy crowded into the seat with his mother and sister. The seat beside me was empty. I'd scared the poor child. Was I that scary?

I got up, went to the restroom, and looked in the mirror. As I washed my hands, what I took for normal was not. No one walked around with a bandaged nose, a bandage across the cheeks and tied at the back of the head. I took it off and I looked again.

No, I cannot go out there with this scarred–up nose and crooked nostril, and one sort of tucked up under the nose. On went the bandage again, and I pulled the curls on the back of my head, over the tied-up bandage. Then I wiped my tears and went out.

As I sat back down, the little boy looked sheepishly over at me. I smiled at him, and he looked away. Then the little girl stood up, came across the aisle, and asked if she could sit with me. I nodded, and she smiled and sat down with a wide grin on her face. She turned to her brother and said, "See? She is okay. She is not a bandit."

That was when I learned that not all people were offended by me. Children simply spoke what was on their minds. They did not intentionally mean to be cruel, like some adults did.

The lady and her two children soon left the train, and more people got on. There was the usual hustle and bustle at every station we stopped: people getting on and off, suitcases and packages loaded and unloaded. For a few stops it was interesting, and then it was repetitive.

The scenery was flat land; some were green fields, and some were yellow, but many more were brown with little scrubby bushes. Here and there, I saw a row of trees with a house among them. I heard someone say the trees were for a windbreak because the wind blew a lot here. Then there would be little creeks with water in them; these had trees and bushes growing all along them. I saw an occasional horse, a few cows, and sheep.

Sometimes I saw people bent over digging or pulling what looked like roots of trees or bushes; it looked like hard work. Once I saw a man plowing a field, and a donkey was pulling the plow. He had a lot done. Next to that was a beautiful green field. He was successful in his endeavors.

In the back of my mind, I thought, *Some of my relatives who stayed in Saskatchewan and got land to farm must be working hard to make a go of it.* I said a little prayer for them all.

I slept occasionally, used the restroom, and washed up. Then I went back to my seat. The conductor brought water, and I drank some and ate a bit of cheese, nuts, cookies, bread, and fruit. Gretchen had asked the ladies in the kitchen to pack food for my long trip.

There were longer stops at Regina and larger towns. Soon the conductor announced that we were pulling into Calgary. There were pens of all kinds of cows—cattle, I was told. They were to be taken to a slaughterhouse in Lethbridge. All this was new to me. I was happy I did not eat meat, and I felt sorry for the cows, pigs, and chickens. They did not have much of a future.

Calgary was a bigger town than most we had stopped at. I sat and looked out, and the ladies wore beautiful dresses. I noticed a great deal of the men wore suits, ties, and hats. Some nodded their heads as they walked by others. Some took off their hats and nodded. How interesting, and so polite.

Some people got off the train and then got back on, eating ice cream piled on what looked like cardboard shaped into cones. The ice cream looked good, and so I got up to buy one too. The conductor called to me from the end of the car, and I turned around. He came striding toward me with the biggest ice cream cone I'd ever seen. It had white, pink, and chocolate ice cream piled up on top of each other. I tried to pay him for it, but he shook his head no, and I thanked him. It was delicious, and I licked and savored every bite. I ate it quickly because it started to melt.

Soon the whistle blew. I jumped every time it did. We pulled out of Calgary for my last leg of the trip. I got excited and worried. I was excited to see the family and relatives. I was worried what they expected, and what they would think of my face. What would they say? How would I handle everything?

I took everything that was handed to me. I remembered Irena's words and her advice. How I missed everyone in Brandon. I sort of wished I was going back there instead of where I was heading, toward all the uncertainties.

I looked out of the window again. The flat fields had changed to little hills, and then the little hills changed into bigger ones. In the distance I saw towering mountains, and some had white caps on them. I did not mind snow, if I had warm clothes. The snow was high up on the mountaintops. Never in my life had I seen such high mountains. I wondered, *How are we going to get through these high mountains?* Soon the train chugged into the mountains and the thick forests. There were such big trees that I was sure I could not put my arms around them. They were so thick and lush, and all the shrubs were green. Out the window, I saw three deer, a mama and two little ones with spots on their backs. I got a glimpse of a big brown bear with two cute cubs.

As we came to a mountain, I thought, *How are we going to go over it?* One side was rock cliff, and the other was a river. We could not go around it. All of a sudden, everything was dark and then it was light again. We went *through* the mountain! There was a big tunnel in the mountain.

I saw things on my journey to British Columbia that I'd never dreamed of, and it was very interesting.

As I went along my way, my heart started to pound. It was not excitement but fear of the unknown. I did not know how I was going to cope with everything.

Here it was, 1910, and I was heading to Ootishenia. I was informed there was no such stop on the railroad there. It would have to be Castlegar, and then the train went to either Grand Forks or branched off to Trail. But I need not have worried; there to meet me was Papa, Mama, Nellie, and Noora, who was now eleven years old.

Noora informed me, "Call me Annie. Noora is too childish." It was the first thing she said to me.

We all hugged, kissed, and cried. There were other people staring at us.

Papa gathered my possessions and my trunk, which was fairly heavy. A nice man helped him lift it into a wagon that Papa had borrowed, and we were away on the last leg of my journey. Shortly we were in Kinnaird, and the team of horses was skittish about getting on the ferry. Then we were in Waterloo on the other side, which was Ootishenia. We went up the river bank, past a small cemetery, past what was called the hospital, and past a row of small houses. Soon we pulled up in front of our little log house at the edge of the village that was newly constructed. Men, women, and children gathered out of curiosity; some gave me hugs and were truly happy to see me.

Some were curious and nosy. Some made comments about the clothes I wore because I had not worn the Russian outfits while I was away. On the train, I had worn a plain navy dress made from a rayon crepe material, high-heeled shoes, and a warm and wooly sweater. I heard whispered comments about my clothes and the shoes, some of which were not very nice.

When we got inside, Papa said, "Ignore all the remarks. You will hear many. Some are jealous, and many are vicious gossip. But maybe wear the old Russian outfits, as before."

My sadder life started.

Papa had added a second story to the log house he had previously constructed. That was the living quarters for us girls. It was a surprise for me. My sisters were so excited to have me back home. They had so many things to tell me and were full of questions about my last four years. We laughed, cried, and got reacquainted.

Mama was so happy to see me. Everyone was so worried about me over the four years that I had been away. Grandfather and Grandmother cried. My aunts were there, as were all the cousins who'd come to British Columbia. There was so much to catch up on. So many things had changed.

Everyone was happy about their gifts and thanked me for them over and over again; they had never been given anything before. They all wanted to see my nose and asked why I did not want to take off the bandages, if it was not sore anymore. Some questions were so hard to answer, and I had to convince them that I was all right.

I had to get out of my dress and wear the regular skirts and blouses I'd used before, like all the girls and women did. Everyone here criticized my "English" dresses. Mind you, everyone would criticize everything I did: my clothes, my shoes, and my nose most of all.

It did not take us long to find out. The neighbors were at our house in no time. Some brought well wishes, dishes of food, or little goodies. Most were there out of curiosity and nosiness. Some were very mean with remarks about my lack of nose.

I ran upstairs and cried. I heard my grandfather chastising some of the mean, gossipy women. "How can you be so unkind, after what she went through for the past four years? All the pain and uncertainties she had to endure alone. Now you are making it more painful for her. Why?"

They were Christians. May God forgive them, because it was hard for me to accept this and forgive them. From that day forward, I had to have courage.

I asked my parents, "Where can I get this courage? I wish I had never come to British Columbia, even if it is a beautiful place."

I was so exhausted and did not eat the nice supper Mama had prepared. I had Nellie bring me a pail of warm water, took off my bandage, washed my face, took a face cloth from my trunk, and washed myself the best I could. Nellie kindly washed my back. Feeling refreshed, I snuggled down on my newly made feather bed and fell into a dreamless sleep.

I woke to a sunny morning with sisters Annie and Nellie looking down at me and smiling. They hugged me and told me they loved me and would try to protect me from all the gossip.

The Lordly

The next day, Peter the Lordly Verigin sent word with one of the ladies that I was to go to his house to see him, because he wanted a word with me. I did not know the man, but I'd heard of him, so I was afraid. Would he send me away? Would he be mean and unkind like the people had been yesterday?

My mother and Nellie walked down the road with me to a large, beautiful white house. There were flowers all over the large yard, which overlooked the Columbia River. It was upriver from the ferry landing. I was told it belonged to a mining boss who'd left Canada and gone back to live in the United States of America—and he was not coming back. This place was on the allotted land that the Doukobours got, so it was an ideal place for the Lordly to live.

As we neared the house, some of the workers came out and greeted us politely. The Lordly had servants who showed us into the house. We sat and waited until Peter Verigin came out of another room. He greeted me with a little hug and told my mother he wanted to speak to me alone. Mama looked at me and then got up slowly to go outside. I heard her talking to some ladies.

When we were alone, Peter the Lordly asked me how my trip was, how my stay in Brandon had worked out, and where I got the money to stay somewhere during and after my operations. I told him the truth. I'd ironed, scrubbed floors, and interpreted for Ukrainian ladies. Of course, he wanted to know how I learned the English language, I did not tell him about sneaking out to learn from Miss Simmons in Pelly. I spoke about Mrs. Graham having a tutor for her son, and she insisted I learn while I had the chance; it was necessary for me to converse with the family and the staff at the hospital.

He told me I was a brave young lady, and I'd done right to fend for myself, but it was going to be a hard grind among our own people. Some could be very mean and vindictive for no reason.

He also asked me to do my share of work in the community, though I did not know what I was to do. He told me to work with my sister in the community gardens. She would tell me what I had to do for four days.

He said, "Then one day you will come to this house and iron my clothes for me and my caretaker. Her name is Nastasia. When there is a shortage of work, you can weave cloth and rugs on a loom set up in one of the other buildings."

That sounded all right to me, but in the back of my mind, I thought, *Why does Nastasia not iron?*

As we headed home along the road, people looked at us. Some peered from their windows, or from behind bushes and trees in their yards. Some were brazen enough to come out to the road in front of us and ask where I'd been and what I'd done to help in the community. Some were mean, as Peter Lordly said they wood be, and they told me not to come near them or their families. I avoided these people at all times.

I went home many times crying my eyes out. One day Grandpa came upon me in that situation, and he put his arms around me and cried with me. If there was something he could do, he said he would do it. He felt so bad for me. "Be brave. Smile when you are hurting. There will always be unkind and mean people in this world. I know you've had more than your share of it. But you have to lift your chin up and be brave. I realize how hard it was for you before, and some things do not go away. Cry if you must. Then wipe your tears, wash your face, and smile. I know it will be rough going, but you are strong and a better person than some of these mean, unkind people, and you can do it."

I tried very hard every day. Each day brought me something else to worry about. Life was hard, but life went on regardless of how I felt.

The community work was backbreaking and very tiring. We weeded, hoed, raked, did assorted field work, and grew our own vegetable gardens besides the community ones. After the fields, we would come home and work some more. At the end of the day, I was ready to drop.

Often Grandpa would light the banya, bathhouse, and we would wash up, wash our clothes by hand, hang them out to dry, bring them in, and iron them with sad irons heated on the stove. We did not live in a communal house, and I understood it was because of me being different. We lived in a log house, and the grandparents lived in a small house constructed by my father. My grandparents were old and could not do much. We lived and ate the meals Mama prepared from food from our garden. We put food away for the winter, like potatoes, carrots, beets, and cabbage.

We existed.

On Saturdays, I went to the Lordly's house to iron his many suits of linen clothes and Nastasia's many skirts and blouses and zanaveskas (aprons) with lots of ribbons and lace. The pleats were hard to get smooth, but due to my previous practice of ironing, I did a quick and thorough job. The weaving was a switch from my routine work.

After I finished my ironing and hanging up the clothes, Papa made wooden hangers. I explained to Papa what the hangers looked like at the doctor's house. These hangers worked well to keep clothes from creasing, and it kept them looking nice.

Peter the Lordly was impressed with things I did, and so was his lady friend and caregiver, Nastasia.

If the sun shone, I hurried and got everything done so that I could go outside. The house was different. It was built by a previous owner but was now on community property. It had a veranda around three sides of it, as well as climbing sweet-smelling roses in white, pink, and yellow. The yard had more assorted flowers than I had ever seen before, and they were beautiful. There were assorted trees, including cherry, apple, peach, pear, and mulberry.

The grounds were taken care of by men and women designated to do these jobs. I felt privileged to be able to work there and walk around the grounds. Some days I would go to the banks of the Columbia River, sit, watch it, and dream.

On Sundays we would dress in our Sunday best. I was happy to have brought home for Mama, Grandma, and my sisters some ribbon and lace. These were put on the aprons and looked nice. We were teased and made fun of, but it was jealousy and envy.

We walked over three miles to meetings and prayer groups, where we would worship and pray. My favorite was the harmonic singing—not the prayer songs, but the old folk songs. Peter the Lordly would lecture the people on how to be good to one another, and to not be mean and envious of other. They should not be quarrelsome, but should love one another.

That was short-lived. It lasted until the meetings were over. On the way home, some of the people were mean to me, even pushing and poking me around when Papa was not watching. I tried to be brave and save my tears for when I was alone and no one would see.

Our Neighbors

One day I sat behind the house, crying. A kindly, blond, curly-haired gentleman bent down and touched me on the head. "Do not cry. Everything will be all right."

When I looked up, I saw two beautiful, blonde, curly-haired girls, both smiling at me.

"I am Roger Swanson. This is Rebecca, my daughter, and the younger is Selena. My wife, Edna, is at home; she is not well. I was told that you understand the English language. Can you please come and help me with my wife and children? The community has excused you from the garden and field work. I have gone over your head and got permission from the community and your parents. Please do not say no—we need you. Please say you will come. I will pay you for your work. I have to return to work and cannot leave my family without help."

I did not realize the Swansons were our next-door neighbors. I told my parents and then left with Roger and the girls. At their house, I found a total mess. Most every dish in the kitchen was dirty, the floors had not been washed for weeks, and the dog and cat were underfoot and hungry. I fed them with some stuff I found in the cupboard; it did not look edible, but the animals thought it was great.

I went into the bedroom and met Edna. She tried to smile but did not quite master it. She looked so sick and weak. I fluffed up her not-clean pillow and told her I would be back.

I lit the stove, put on a couple of pots of water, went out to their vegetable garden, and found some vegetables among the weeds. The girls were at my heels and tried to be helpful. They were very curious about me, but I told them we would talk later. First we had to get some food. I wanted to make some soup for their mom.

Roger was outside chopping wood. I put assorted vegetables into a pot of water, and I found a bottle of milk that was not sour; they had a cow and fresh milk. I poured some into the pot, took out the potatoes and mashed them, put in some butter, and made a healthy soup that smelled good.

While the soup was boiling on the stove, I went into the bedroom with a basin of water and a nice-smelling soap I had found in the cupboard. I helped Edna to the commode—thank the Lord they had one. It was not too clean but was handy. I got her back in bed; washed Edna's face, neck, arms, and back; sat her up; pulled down her gown; and told her to try to wash the rest of herself. In the meantime, I found clean bedding. I put on a clean pillow case, rolled up the sheet to half of the bed, finished washing Edna's feet and legs, made her lie back, moved her over to the clean half of the bed, and pulled the sheet over to the side she had lay on. She tried to smile.

The soup was about ready. The girls found some dried

bread, and I cut it up, put the bread cubes on a baking sheet, and made croutons that were nicely browned in the oven. I made the girls wash their hands and face and had them sit down at a cleaned spot at the table. I filled two large bowls of soup and set them down in front of them.

Their father walked in with a load of wood, and he put it into the wood box. He made a comment about the great smell as I set a bowl of soup topped with croutons at another cleaned spot at the table. He and the girls ate.

I filled another bowl and took it in to Edna. I had to help her eat because she had no strength. She had a fever and had trouble breathing. I felt so sorry for her. I got cold well water and a clean towel, and I mopped her fevered brow. She dropped off to sleep.

Roger thanked me and made me sit and have some soup too. He said he had to go to work that evening; he was getting a ride to a logging camp, across the river. "A friend will row me across and bring back the boat. If you need to take Edna to the doctor in Trail, the friend will row you over. You can catch the bus that goes by at ten o'clock every morning. The girls can stay at our friend's place until you get back."

I thought, *Oh, Lord. What did I get myself into?* I got scared, but these poor people needed help.

Roger checked on Edna, who was still sleeping, and he left to cross the river and go to work.

I started in one corner of the bedroom and cleaned. I washed everything, put dirty clothes into a pile to be washed, heated water, and scrubbed floors. Everything smelled nice and clean when I was finished. Edna slept on, under my scrutinizing eye. The girls helped with anything I asked, and I got them to wash the dirty dishes in the kitchen.

Even the animals stayed out of our way. I heard the cow mooing, and she needed to be milked, but I had never done that. I sent the girls to get my father, and he milked the cow. Tomorrow, I would watch and do it myself.

I cleaned the girls' room, changed the bedding, piled clothes into different colors to be washed, heated more water, and put the clothes into large tubs to soak. I was so tried, and it was dark, but I could not stop.

I made the girls wash and go to bed. I could hear Edna coughing, and so I went in and took care of her toilet necessities. She was still breathing harshly and coughing. I warmed some milk and made her drink it. Then I put cool clothes on her because she had a fever and did not look good. The girls came in and said good night to her, and Edna commented on how good they smelled and looked.

After they went to bed and Edna fell asleep, I got a comforter and bedded down beside her on the floor, so I could look after her should she need me. That was after I scrubbed some clothes and hung them up to dry. I did have a purpose in life: someone needed me. I slept so soundly that night, as did Edna.

I was awakened to roosters crowing. The girls were up and showed me how much feed to give to the chickens. Papa came over and milked the cow.

Edna was awake and felt as feverish as the day before. As we did her toiletry and washing, we decided she needed to see a doctor. But how was she to make it up and down the riverbank to and from the boat, and to the bus? Papa went to get Ray, their friend. Between Papa and Ray, we would manage. I got the girls their breakfast of porridge and milk. Edna had a bit, and I ran home and got a dress for myself, something I had worn in Brandon. I grabbed a few pieces of dried bread, and we were on our way.

Ray's wife looked after the girls. They looked so sad and scared.

Papa and Ray carried Edna to the boat. When we got across the river, they helped get her up the hill to the road, where she sat on a rock while we waited for the bus. Ray said, "My wife can look after the girls. Your father can milk the cow and feed the chickens, the dog, and the cat. Do not worry."

I replied, "Oh, dear. How can we not worry?"

That was when we thought of money for the bus. Thank goodness Edna had thought of it before, because she had some money in her sweater pocket, done up with a safety pin so as not to lose it.

I did not know at that time that this was the start of me being an interpreter for the Russian people who did not speak English and needed medical help. I was a help to the English-speaking ones too.

We got on the bus with the help of Papa and Ray. Edna paid, and we were on our way to Trail. It was the first time for me. It was a long, windy road, but we finally arrived, going through the smelter. It was very big and smelly, but it employed a great deal of people.

As we got down the hill and into town, I saw the hospital. It was a three-story building. The bus went by and went three more streets farther. How was I going to get Edna to the hospital? She was having trouble breathing. I got up and tried to help her up, to no avail. Finally, a kindly gentleman lifted her up and carried her off the bus. Now what? The man stood right beside us, and half walked, half carried Edna to the hospital. I thanked him.

At the hospital, finally the doctor came and took her into another room. He told me to come along, and after examining her, he told me she was to be admitted to the hospital. She was really bad and had pneumonia. She needed medication and oxygen.

I did not know what to do, so I signed my name that I was admitting her. What was I to do? The doctor told me to go home. There was a bus back to Nelson, through Castlegar, that afternoon. Edna gave me money for the return trip and more. After I saw her settled comfortably in bed, she was given oxygen and medication. The nurses and doctor were really nice. Edna was going to be all right. I was told she would be in the hospital for a week or so.

I said good-bye to Edna, and she told me to go to Woolworth's and get something for the girls, and to give them both a hug from her. She trusted that I would do all right.

I went outside, and tears welled in my eyes. I did not cry—I was brave, I was strong. Someone needed me, and so I was strong.

I followed Edna's directions got to Woolworth's. There was so much stuff, and I was practical. I got the girls pretty sweaters and little Kewpie dolls. I then went to the bus stop and waited.

I was so hungry; all I'd had was a slice of bread that

day. I saw people eating ice cream cones, but I did not dare spend Edna's money on that. Sitting beside me was a lady, and she watched me take the money out and put it back. She got an ice cream cone for herself and another for me. I shook my head no, but she held it out to me. I took it and said thanks. There were kind and caring people in this world!

Soon the bus came. I got on the bus, leaned my head against the window, and fell asleep from pure exhaustion. The next thing I knew, the bus driver said we were in Kinnaird, my stop. I got out.

As I hurried down the pathway to the river, I remembered no one knew I was coming home. How was I going to get across? Pretty soon I was at the bank of the Columbia. It had never looked so wide before. It was dusk. I saw someone on the other side, and so I shouted. They answered that they would try to get someone to row across and get me. It was becoming dark, and behind me I heard the howl of a coyote. I was told that there were bears also, though I never saw any. I was petrified. Soon I saw a lantern going down the path to the river. Someone was coming to get me.

I was so thankful to see the lantern and boat drawing closer. Soon, I heard the thump of the boat on the rocks, and I headed to the water. It was Swanson's friend, Ray. I thanked him over and over. He said, "You were a brave person to take Edna to the hospital. The girls are waiting. Tomorrow I will get word to Roger about his wife." He thanked me very much, because I'd probably saved her life.

I stayed and cleaned the Swansons' house from top to bottom. I cleaned their chicken coop, cleaned their barn, and made sure everyone and every creature was fed. I did not know how to cook their meat dishes, but that was not a problem—the girls loved the vegetarian food I cooked them. They had beautiful blonde, naturally curly hair, and I combed and braided it for them. They missed their parents but were happy I was with them.

On the second day, Papa said it was time I learned to milk Josie, the cow. I washed her teats, dried them, and tried pulling. Nothing came, and I tried harder, but still nothing. Finally with a squeeze and a pull, I got milk. By the time I finished, my hands were ready to fall off. Next time it got easier, and Josie got used to me. She turned around and gave my kerchief a lick.

Three days later, Ray came to tell me Edna was feeling much better, and Roger would bring her home when she was released from the hospital, but he would need my help. Saturdays I could do my ironing, and Sunday I could go to the meetings. "Stay on and help them, please," said Ray.

Some days I was so tired that I was happy to hit my pillow. I slept in the girls' room on a bench that folded out from the wall. I called it my shelf, and the girls laughed. They loved their new sweaters and the little dollies. They could hardly wait for their mom to come home.

On Saturday, Ray rowed across the river. Soon he and Roger were on either side of Edna, carrying packages. The animals were so happy, and the girls were ecstatic. Everyone was smiling and crying. Edna was wide-eyed and excited about how nice the house and garden looked. "Everything is so clean and orderly!" she commented.

The girls were anxious to show her their room, and they promised to keep it tidy in order to help their mother.

That afternoon I went home with money in my apron pocket. Grandpa said I would have to give all of it to the community fund. Why? They had not done the work, and they did not get me the job. He still insisted.

I went to do my ironing at the Lordly house. When I finished, I gently knocked on the door of Peter the Lordly. A gruff voice bid me to come in. "Mankiya, nice to see you. Are you all right?"

I replied, "Yes."

"What seems to be the problem?" he asked.

"I have a dilemma with my grandfather. I have not worked in the gardens and fields for a while. I helped at the Swanson house. Mr. Swanson paid me some money. Grandfather says I have to give it to the community fund. The dilemma is, do I? All of it, or a portion of it?"

"How much did he pay you?" he asked.

"I got seven dollars and fifty cents," I answered.

"Did you work hard?"

"Yes, I worked hard. I cleaned up the house, cleaned out the barn, weeded the garden, cooked food for the girls, saw to it they had their baths, cleaned their clothes, and saw to it the cow and pets were fed. It was the hardest I have ever worked."

"All right. You also need clothes, bandages for your face, and shoes for your feet. Your few dollars will not help the community. Keep it all for yourself. I understand Mrs. Swanson is not well. You are excused from the community work. You can work for her until she is well. The money you earn is yours to keep—do not let your grandfather tell you different. If he does, tell him to come see me. You will not be getting your share from the community gardens, because you will not be working there. That way the neighbors will have nothing to complain about. If anyone complains or gives you a rough time, come and see me. You can go now."

I Can Do It

I left with a lighter heart and a brisker walk. I skipped on the way home, in a good mood. Out of the bushes came a scared voice: it was Aloshenka Charnov. He was a bit slow but harmless, I'd been told. It was a warm afternoon, but he had a long coat on. Of course, I was nosy and commented on the long coat.

He said, "Oh, I am so sore."

"Why?" I inquired.

"It was so embarrassing. I sat down by the river to have a dump. There were some soft-leaved bushes to wipe my behind with. Oh, it was the wrong thing to do. They were poison ivy, I think it is called. I am so sore, red, and burning. I cannot have my pants touch my behind. The wool is irritating and makes me itch even more. Oh, I am in agony! What am I to do?"

There I stood, trying not to laugh. I put my hand over my mouth. Finally I said, "Take some baking soda, go into the bathhouse, and make a basin full of warm water and soda. Then sit in it. It may relieve the itch."

I ran on home, giggling. It was something I had not done since I was with my friends in Brandon. It felt so nice that I could still laugh.

I confronted my grandfather for the first time. We still had our differences, and I thought he was too strict. I explained what had transpired at the Lordly's home, adding that it was all right for me to keep the money I'd earned. I still loved him and the rest of the family. I would help with anything I could.

Life went on. I would help Edna and the girls while Roger went to work, and he paid me regularly. My little stash grew, and I kept it on a shelf. Papa made a false front on it, in a tin box; it was my secret hiding place. He and I were the only ones who knew about it.

One day, one of the neighbors who'd been mean to me when I first came to Ootishenia, Hadooka, was in tears. She said, "Mankiya, you have to help me. I need to go to Trail. I have never been there, and I do not know the English language. I need to get my tooth looked at. You have to come with me."

I did not have to go with her, but I did feel sorry for her. She had no friends and was in pain, and I did know what pain was. "Oh, I do not *have* to go with you. You forgot to say sorry, and there is that word: please," I said. I tried not to sound malicious, as she had before.

"Please, please. I am so sorry I said nasty things to you," she begged. "I will pay your bus fare and everything."

I agreed to go the next day. She got Ray to row us across the river, and she paid our bus fare. I brought her a towel and wet it in the river to cool her bad tooth. She kept turning the towel to the cooler side as we rode the bus to the dentist. When we got there, I inquired where the dentist office was. We got there and had to sit and wait until the dentist was finished with his patient.

I went in with her to the room where the dental chair was. She was terrified, and so I consoled her the best I could. Upon examination, the dentist said she needed to get the tooth pulled; it would not hurt after the freezing. He gave her the needle and froze her gums, and then he decided it should not be pulled but filled instead. He told her it would cost eight dollars. She turned away and pulled up her skirt. Attached around her waist was a pocket where she kept her money, hiding it from everyone. She paid the dentist, and we left.

She said she was thirsty and hungry because she had not eaten for two days due to her tooth. The dentist told her not to chew on that tooth for several hours. We went into the Blue Bird Restaurant a few doors past the bus depot, and it smelled good.

We had vegetable soup and crackers. Haniya had never had crackers before, so I gave her mine too. I took her to see some of the stores, like the company store and Woolworth's. She was excited about everything and even forgot about her sore tooth when the freezing wore off.

Soon we were on our way home. Haniya had made arrangements with Ray to row us back across the river. Before I left her at her door, she went into her money pocket and gave me two dollars. I did not refuse to take it or ask her where she got her money; I simply thanked her. She was so thankful that I believed I'd acquired a new friend. Without her previous bad remarks, it would be a bit easier to live in the community.

News travelled fast. I had people asking me why I'd taken Haniya to Trail. I felt it was not my business to say anything about other people in the community. That way, people trusted me and confided in me. If they needed help to go to the doctor or dentist, they would not hesitate to ask me to come with them and translate for them. It was all right for me. I still did housework and babysat for the Swansons.

One day, Roger came over to our place with a new camera. He wanted us to pose for a picture. My grandparents adamantly refused. I told them to stand and watch; they did not have to get their pictures taken. Nellie, Annie, and I posed while they watched. Then we all stood around them, including the parents, as Roger took more pictures. They were not really aware because they'd never had their pictures taken before.

When Roger brought the pictures over two weeks later, they were flabbergasted. They were looking at themselves in the pictures, and nothing bad happened to them. That was very exciting for everyone. Roger made extra pictures for us to send to our relatives in Russia and Saskatchewan.

I wrote a nice letter and sent two pictures to Uncle Misha and his family, because we still had his address in Russia. I was told at the Castlegar post office that it would take many weeks for them to receive the letter. It cost me eleven cents to send it.

It was a long walk to get to the little village of Castlegar. I met with the people who wanted to be independent of the community, Fomies. They opened up a little general store. Ray would row me across the river for ten cents, and then I learned I could board the train and go to the village for another ten cents. I would walk back.

Eremenko's store was a bit bigger, and it had many

things in it. Mrs. Eremenko often needed help mending things, and she said she was not good at things like that; neither was her daughter-in-law from Vancouver. Their only son had married her not too long ago, according to Mrs. Eremenko, and the girl was useless but was beautiful. Their son was a short, bald man even though he was young. There was talk that he was a drunk and was lucky Larrisa had married him.

There was the post office, as well as a grocery store owned by another man who had left the community. There were two shoemakers, and one was reasonably priced; I had a heel put back on one of my shoes. Next door to the post office was a clothing store with beautiful women's clothes, some men's clothes, and shoes. I would sometimes go in and look, because the community did not allow us to wear what they called English clothes. I still had my clothes from Brandon, and someday I would wear them again.

There was even a hair place where the lady cut and styled women's hair. Imagine that! I trimmed my own bangs and hair.

One day Axeenya, a beautiful lady in our community, came to me in tears. She'd lost her husband in a logging accident, when a tree fell on him. She had five children, and the oldest was eleven, but the youngest was just a year old. She said she was pregnant and needed help. I told her I would help her with the children, but that was not what she wanted. She wanted me to go to Castlegar with her. I did as she asked.

She wanted me to go to the drug store and translate to the druggist. She told him she needed some bark, to abort the baby on the way. He asked how far along she was and whether her husband knew about this. I translated her answers, and he did not hesitate to give her the bark, but he warned that she should not come back to him and hold him responsible if she ran into problems. He added she should have a hot sauna before and after.

I felt embarrassed and very guilty; it brought back memories of Fesha in Brandon. Fesha had been all right, so I made it a point to mind my own business.

Next time I saw Axeenya, she was smiling and winked at me. I guess things had worked for her. God forgive her. I felt I was responsible for misdemeanors like this.

Many ladies did not trust the midwife, Natasha. Yes, she was still a midwife, and maybe she was good at delivering children. She would come to me to take them to a doctor or to the drug store for medication. Many had to have their teeth taken care of. I did not refuse the ladies anything like that. I did not mind translating for them, and most of them would pay me, though it was little because they had very little.

Working Outside the Community

One day, Mr. Delong came to our door. He said he was running an experimental farm a short way from Trail and needed help. He wanted me to help with the housework, because his wife had fallen down and hurt her back, and she could hardly walk. After a few moments of conversing with Papa, I went with him across the river on Ray's boat. Then we went up the hill but not to the highway and the bus. We went to the little red train station, and soon we heard the train chugging along. Mr. Delong got out the little white flag, and the engineer tooted twice to tell us he noticed and was stopping for us. The little flag was hung back up inside, and we got on the train and headed toward Trail.

We went on through Blueberry Creek, China Creek, and Genelle. We stopped on a flat spot shortly after and got out. Mr. Delong took my little bundle of clothes and started up the hillside path.

Soon we were on a nice green farm, with beautiful gardens that had a wide assortment of vegetables, many of which I had never seen before. We went into the house, and two dirty-faced children met us. I was introduced to Doug, seven years old, and Valerie, nine years old. They took me into the bedroom to meet Mrs. Delong, who lay among unclean bedding and didn't move much.

She gave me a few instructions as to what I was to do and then closed her eyes. I heard her say to her husband, "She is so tiny. Will she manage?"

I got my apron from my little pack and attacked the kitchen, I started with the table and cupboards, and I put dishes in large wash basins to soak. Valerie was trying to help because her father had told her to do so. Doug had to go work in the large fields and garden.

Soon there was some semblance of order showing. I put water on to boil on the large cast-iron cook stove. It had a tank with pipes into the stove to heat it, and soon warm water came out of the tap in the sink. Valerie was very helpful in showing me all the new things.

We went out to the garden to dig potatoes and pick other vegetables. Soon we had a meal of soup, fried potatoes, green beans, and beet greens, at which Valerie looked rather doubtfully.

When the food was ready, I took some soup in to Mrs. Delong. She was famished and slurped it up quickly. I took her the vegetable meal, which she devoured as quickly. I also made her a cup of tea, and she sat back and sipped contentedly.

Mr. Delong and Doug did not come in until it was dark. They carried in a pail of milk and told me it had to be separated. Separated? What was separated?

Valerie showed me how. The separator stood on a cupboard in the kitchen, and it needed a good wash—as did everything else. It was neat the way milk went to one spout, and the cream went through another.

They all sat down and made me sit with them and have the meal I and Valerie had prepared earlier. Then Valerie and I cleaned up the dishes, cleared a shelf to put them on, and cleaned up the table.

I took apart the milk separator and washed it, rinsed it with hot water, and checked all the other moving mechanisms. I washed and scrubbed the cupboard on which it stood. Valerie showed me the ice box the milk went into so it would not sour.

Mr. Delong went in to talk to his wife after he told the kids to go to bed. He came out with a pillow, a sheet, and a blanket for me. He showed me another bedroom that would be mine while I stayed there. The floor needed sweeping and a good washing, and there were no curtains on any windows.

Morning came soon, and I was still tired. Valerie knocked on the door and told me they had to go weed before they could have breakfast and get ready for school. I got up, lit the stove, and got water ready for a wash for Mrs. Delong. Soon I went in, helped her up to the commode, helped her wash her face, and used a small towel on her back. Her back was black and blue where she'd hurt it, and it was also scabbed and sore-looking.

In one of the cupboard drawers, I found clean sheets and pillowcases. She was happy to lie back into a clean bed. I went into the kitchen, made her some porridge, and brought it in with milk cool from the ice box.

Soon the rest of the family came in for their washes and breakfast. Mr. Delong had to catch a bus to go to work, and the children got on a bright orange school bus to get to school in Trail.

I looked in on Mrs. Delong, and she was sound asleep, so I got busy. First I separated the milk and put it in the ice box. Then I washed the separator and the dishes. I made sure the wood box was full, to keep the stove going for hot water all day.

In the shed behind the house, I found washtubs, took all the bedding I'd stripped earlier, and went into the children's room. It was a room divided in half so each could have privacy. I took their dirty bedding and dirty clothes, sorting them into whites, colors, and darks. I took all the laundry to the shed, got pails of water, and put the clothes in the tubs to soak.

I came back in the house and checked on Mrs. Delong. She was still asleep, so I tackled the kitchen, starting in one corner. I found a hard-bristle brush in the shed and scrubbed and scrubbed. Then I got clean water and did some more scrubbing. I could see a pretty peach-colored wood halfway up the wall. The top was actually a cream color, and the cupboards were peach with cream shelving. It was very pretty.

I was so busy that I lost track of time. Soon, Mrs. Delong was calling me; she needed help to use the commode again. I straightened up her bed while she was up, and when she got back into bed, I went out and got her a sliced hard-boiled egg sandwich and some leftover soup from the night before. I washed her face and back again. I did not like the looks of her scratches; they were sore-looking. I told her I would be in the shed doing the laundry, and she should shout if she needed me. Soon she was snoozing again.

I had a long line of sheets, pillowcases, and towels

hanging on the line, whipping around in the gentle breeze. It was a nice, sunny day, and I put the children's clothing on the bushes around the house. In the meantime, I went back to the kitchen and scrubbed some more.

I thought it would be a good idea to clean the children's rooms before they got back from school. I swept and washed the floors, and they were a pretty light gray.

I found two sad irons and put them on the stove to heat them. Then I ironed the children's clothes. As they dried, I put clean sheets and pillowcases on their beds. The blankets would get washed next time. I lined up their clean clothes at the foot of their beds. I then washed their doors before I closed them.

Back to Mrs. Delong. When I looked at her back, it was starting to ooze and looked infected in spots. I went out into the green grass that grew around the house and found the leaf I was looking for. I did not know what it was called at the time, but I later learned it was plantain (just a weed).

I took it in and showed Mrs. Delong that I was going to crush it and put it on the oozing spots on her back, as my grandmother had done for us. She was so sore that she did not care what I did to her. I gently swabbed her back with cool water and then applied the leaves and a clean piece of gauze I found on one of the shelves. She lay on her side and was soon sound asleep.

The children came home and ran into the house. They had forgotten I was there. They came in the kitchen and then stopped and stared around in amazement. After that, they went to see their mother, who was still asleep. Next they headed to their bedrooms, and before they touched the door, they both rushed me and gave me a big hug. They whooped when they walked into their rooms and saw clean bedding, clean clothes, and a nice floor.

"Oh, Mary. What did you do?" they inquired. "Everything looks so nice!"

Their mother awoke and called them, reminding them they had to do their work in the fields. I had boiled extra eggs, so they had a snack of eggs, crackers, and milk. Soon they were happily running to do their jobs.

Mrs. Delong called me into the bedroom and told me there was beef steak wrapped in brown paper in the bottom of the ice box. I was supposed to fry it up for dinner. That was when I informed her that I was a vegetarian, had never cooked or eaten beef, and did not know how. She told me what I was to do.

I took some water out to the children, after giving some to their mother. They were all smiles when I arrived; no one ever did that for them. On the way back, I dug new potatoes, picked some peas and shelled them, and went back in the kitchen. They were to go with the steak, which I was worried about. How was I going to manage to cook it? I should have visited the Grahams' kitchen in Brandon more often and watched the ladies there cook meat.

When Mr. Delong came home from work, he told me he would not be in until dark because there was a lot of cultivating to do in the garden. He poked his head in the door to tell me this, and then he did a double take. He noticed how clean and bright the room looked. "Oh, Mary, we have had many workers, and no one did all this.

They had to be told what to do all the time. Nobody did all this. Thank you, thank you!"

His wife called him from the bedroom, and he went in for a few minutes before he went out to the fields. I looked in on her, changed her leaves and gauze, and bathed her back with cool water; it looked so much better. The oozing was stopping, so maybe the leaves did work.

That evening the children separated the milk and took apart the separator to wash. The table was all set, and the vegetables were all ready. I put the meat on the pan to cook just as they walked in. When it was ready, the father served the children and himself, and he made up a plate for his wife, which I took in. She smiled at the plate and said it looked good, but I was to go and eat with the rest of the family.

After the washing and cleanup, I dropped into bed without noticing that I had had no time to clean up my own bedroom.

Morning came early again, with the same hectic rushing around. The children had to get up at daybreak and put in hours of work before breakfast or going to school. I felt sorry for them. The parents were also hardworking.

Mr. Delong went to work after the milk, Mrs. Delong, and the children were taken care of. I decided to make some homemade bread. I found all the ingredients for it and a large enamel kneading bread pan. I got everything ready and mixed, and I left it to rise.

I looked in on Mrs. Delong. She looked better, and her back certainly did. I got a few more leaves and applied them. She said she would sit up for a few minutes and then put herself to bed.

I could only find four bread tins. When the bread was ready to be put into the tins, I found I needed more. I used a pie tin and a square tin I found in the cupboard. I made two small loaves in that one, and the other I filled with some round buns.

I found some of the cream had soured, so I put it in a large jar and shook it until I got butter. I had bread ready to cook and buttermilk. I made blintzes. With that, I picked some strawberries I found in the garden and whipped some fresh cream. That was dinner that night, and everyone enjoyed it.

Mrs. Delong called me and told me she could smell bread cooking. When it was ready, I spread some butter on the small, round buns and took two to her.

The children smelled the bread as soon as they walked in the door and had two slices each before going to the garden.

When Mr. Delong came home, he went straight to the garden, milked the cow, washed his hands and face, and sat down to blintzes, fresh butter, and whipped cream, flavored with a shot of rum because I could not find vanilla. Even Mrs. Delong came to the table, and she was surprised at the brightness of the kitchen. She commented on the previous help never doing such thorough cleaning.

I feared now that Mrs. Delong was feeling better, my job was coming to an end. I stayed for a few more days doing laundry, patching the children's and Mr. Delong's clothes and socks, and helping in the garden. Mrs. Delong was very kind to me, and she prolonged my work a few more days, but she was well now. I had to move on.

She took me to Trail and introduced me to few of her friends. One of them needed help, because she was pregnant and the doctor's orders were that she not do any work for the last two months. I got a new job.

I was to start in two days and was given a room of my own. It was a small but pretty house. Her name was Anita, and his was Lewis Berks. I looked forward to returning in two days' time. Mrs. Delong and I left, and I thanked her for helping me get the job. She told me that I would do well if I did half of the work I'd done at their place. She also wished me luck.

That evening after dinner, the whole family drove me home. They waited by the Columbia River until Ray rowed across to get me. The children were sad and wanted me to go back home with them. I promised I would visit them one day. With sad hugs and teary waves good-bye, they stared up the hill, and Ray rowed the boat across the river. After one more wave, we parted.

All Was Not Well
on the Home Front

On the other side of the river, Ray tied up the boat while I started up the hill. There were kids at the top of the pathway, and they started throwing rocks at me and yelling, "Here comes Miss No-Nose!"

I was hit by a few rocks and was more shocked than hurt. Ray ran up, livid, and he grabbed one of the bigger boys by the scruff of the neck and almost lifted him off his feet. The rest of the kids ran away.

"What is your name?" Ray demanded.

"Yasha," the boy said tearfully.

"Where do you live?"

"Third building, uh, third building on the left, with my grandmother and my brother" was Yasha's answer.

"All right, let's go," said Ray.

That was when Yasha started to cry, "Grandma will kill me!"

"Hope she does," said Ray. "You did not realize that you hurt Mary—not just by throwing rocks but calling her names. Do you not understand she cannot help the way she looks? You are a nice, big boy, but deep inside you are terrible and very ugly. So are your friends. You go and tell them that. Do you understand me?"

The boy nodded.

"Now, run to your grandma and tell her what you did. Tell your friends what I said. I will not let you get away with this name-calling. Just you remember that. That's the end of that nonsense."

Yasha ran off but kept turning around and looking back.

It certainly was not the end. The next day, Mrs. Horkova and a few other ladies came to see me. They were very angry and demanded to have me explain why Ray had grabbed Yasha by the scruff of his neck. I tried to explain, but they started yelling at me. Papa got scared and ran to get Ray. I tried to get them to listen to reason, but they would not. According to them, their boys could do no harm.

Finally, Papa and Ray showed up. Ray held up his arms, and the ladies fell silent. Ray tried to explain that their little boys were troublemakers and cruel, when they had no reason to be. The ladies told him they did not understand English. I tried to translate into Russian, but they would have nothing to do with me.

Ray started in poor Russian, and he told them that if their children did not behave, he would call the police and have them taken away, because they may hurt someone seriously one day. In the meantime he would personally see Peter the Lordly Verigin.

He told the ladies to go home and take care of their sons and grandsons, and to leave me and my family alone.

He told them in English and Russian that they should be ashamed.

The next Sunday, at the general meeting in Brilliant, everyone was there. The Lordly called the five boys, Yasha and his friends, in front of everyone. He shamed them for calling me names and reprimanded them to barn cleanup for throwing rocks at me and Ray. They must not throw rocks at anyone, ever.

The ladies standing by me thought I had told him about this, but I did not. Oh, Lord. What had Ray started? I was so afraid as they started jostling me and poking me in the ribs—discreetly, mind you—and muttering and calling me "No-nose." Some of them even called me a bitch. Why? Because their children were unkind?

I was hurt because the elders were worse than the kids. I ran from the meeting all the way home, over three miles.

Hours later, when the rest of the family got home, they found me covered, head and all, under the blanket, sobbing my head off. What was I to do? I was so hurt I could not talk.

Finally, Grandpa crawled up the stairs to the bedroom I shared with Nellie and Annie. He sat at the edge of the bed and talked to me. "The good Lord let this happen to you. He will also help you get through all this. Look at all the suffering you went through, all the pain you suffered. For some reason, you have to be here. There are good and bad people everywhere. You have experienced meeting the bad, some unintentionally bad like Natasha, and some real bad like Mr. Trafiminkoff. Some are just mischievous like the five boys. You will meet all kinds of people during your lifetime."

He went on. "You will hurt, and you will get over it. You will also meet good people. Some will need you, like the people you work for; their children were kind and concerned about you, as were the parents. You helped them. You have to steel yourself against the remarks wicked people make. Some can be so mean, but there are many good ones among us. I know it is hard to believe. You simply have to discern the different ones, the mean ones, and the ones who mean well."

Work in Trail

The next day, Ray rowed me across the Columbia River. As I walked up the path to the main road to Trail to catch the bus, I glanced back across the river. It was such a beautiful spot—the river, the bank, the trees along the water. Then as my gaze went higher up the bank, there stood a bunch of women and kids. Some were shaking their fists at me, and the kids were hooting and hollering nasty things right in front of their mothers—and without getting reprimanded. As Ray neared the shoreline, they dispersed.

I continued up the pathway on the other side of the river, not looking back and wishing that I did not have to return to that place. The place was lovely, but some of the people were not.

The bus was on time; my little watch that I got in Brandon told me so. The next thing I knew, I was in Trail. I walked up the part of Trail known as the Gulch, with nice homes and lots of gardens. Soon I was at the Burke place. Anita met me at the door with a cheerful smile, and she had a cool glass of lemonade for me. We sat out back under an umbrella; it was a nice backyard, with roses and other flowers everywhere. It was a relaxing place.

Anita informed me the doctor had told her she had to stay in bed the last month and a half of her pregnancy, because she was so small and frail, and there was fear of losing their child, as she had the last two. She was very positive that all would be okay now that I was here to help her, and she thanked me for coming.

Soon we went inside, and she showed me my bedroom. It was airy and bright, with beautiful rugs and a bedspread that matched the chair cover and doilies on the furniture.

Then she opened the closet and told me to hang up my clothes. The bathroom was next door, so I could wash up and then come downstairs to the kitchen. I hung up my clothes, grabbed an apron, went to the bathroom, and washed up. Everything was squeaky clean, and it would be easy to keep it that way.

Downstairs, Anita was in the kitchen preparing a meat dish. I informed her that I was a vegetarian. She said it was no problem, and there were always a lot that I could eat: eggs, cheese, nuts, and a great amount of fruits and vegetables. She would teach me how to cook the meats and fish.

She pointed to the dining room and asked me to set the table. On the table was a beautiful tablecloth and napkins to match. I set the table for the two of them, and when she came in and saw this, she said, "No, put down another setting. You are now our family and will take your meals with us."

That evening when Lewis came home from work, he had a glass of wine. Anita did not drink because of her pregnancy, and so he offered me one. I said, "No, thank you."

We had a pleasant dinner together. They were so nice and polite to me, and I was happy to be there, especially after the previous weekend. I never wanted to go home.

The days that followed were very routine. I woke and took coffee up to Anita. Lewis got his own breakfast and was gone to work. Then Anita got up and had a bath or shower; she did not need my help yet.

I made breakfast for Anita and me. She ate very little, so I tried to fix nice things for her. She was very appreciative. Then I made her bed, vacuumed the floors, and washed the kitchen and bathroom floors.

I would do laundry, but not by hand because they had a washer with wringers on the side. Then I would hang things out to dry; they would dry so much faster than when I wrung them by hand.

I went out and swept the sidewalk in front of the house. People were so friendly and said hello to me. I did not run across mean people like at home. Some would look at me with curiosity, but I think Anita had set them straight before I got there. There was no name-calling or nastiness.

Lewis and Anita drove me to Kinnaird. As prearranged with Ray, he picked me up and rowed me across the river. I did not want to go home for two days, but I did. I returned on the Monday bus.

I got home without insolent behavior from neighbors. I went with the rest of the family to the regular Sunday meeting. I heard no nasty remarks.

On the way home, as we walked, the ladies who lived around our area, caught up with us and started name-calling. They said I thought I was a big shot because

I worked in Trail for the English lady, and that I was nothing but a noseless bitch. They kept this up all the way home. Our family kept quiet, and that made the hecklers even nastier. I was glad to get in the house and away from them.

In the afternoon, I was afraid to go to Peter the Lordly's to iron clothes. Papa walked with me past the nasty neighbors' places, and past the place called the hospital, which was now a communal dining room, where the ladies took turns cooking meals. We lived farther down and so were not included, thank goodness. As we walked by the ladies, they were peering out the windows. We walked past the cemetery; at least those residents did not say or do anything, may they rest in peace.

Papa was a man of few words, so we had no conversation as we walked. Soon we were at the gate to the Lordly's house. The guard greeted us and let us inside. He wanted to know why Papa was with me, and whether I was all right. Papa stayed behind and told him what had happened the other day.

I went to work and ironed and pressed clothes for a few hours. Nastasia soon came into the room with a cool drink made of raspberries for me, and she told me the guard would walk home with me. I should not walk alone anywhere. She also told me there had to be a stop to unkind neighbors. I simply ironed as I listened to her.

That evening when the guard walked with me, there was not anymore name-calling. Even some of the women peeked around from behind the bushes and the corners of houses.

On Monday morning, Ray rowed me across the river.

I got on the bus and went to Trail for the week, and Anita and Lewis drove me back to their house.

I dreaded the Sunday meeting but went anyway. There were no severe incidents that Sunday.

Things went on this way until I had to stay in Trail and be there for Anita in her last days of pregnancy, I enjoyed not having to come home and face the neighbors, even if they had calmed down a bit.

Time went by so fast, and before I knew it, the month and a half had gone by. One afternoon Anita went into the bathroom, and I stayed within hearing distance of her all the time. She called me and told me to telephone the doctor—it was time for the baby to come. The ambulance came in what seemed a few minutes. I was not allowed to go with her, so I locked up and ran to the hospital. First I ran up the hill to tell Lewis that Anita had gone to the hospital. I got there before Lewis, but the nurses made me sit in the waiting room, as they did with Lewis.

Three hours later, the doctor came out carrying a little blue bundle to Lewis. "It's a cute little baby boy. Congratulations."

"How is Anita?" Lewis and I both wanted to know.

"Anita is fine and resting," answered the doctor. "You both can go in and see her. She had a rough time and will need lots of help after she goes home."

We went in to see Anita. She looked so pale and small. Lewis handed me the little baby, and he was such a tiny one. He kissed Anita and held her gently as she dozed.

The nurse came and took the baby from my arms, Anita woke up and smiled at Lewis and at me. "I did it.

He is alive, thanks to all the help Mary gave me." She smiled and fell into an exhausted sleep.

I went to fix dinner for Lewis, and he was so excited when he got home. He was happy that his wife and baby were both all right. "You will stay with us until Anita is stronger. Please do not leave us until later," Lewis said, worried that I would now go home. I told him I would stay as long as they needed my help, and I did.

Mama and baby Eric came home. Anita was weak, and Eric needed a lot of care and clean diapers. I washed, cooked, and cleaned as before. Anita and Lewis depended on me for a lot of things, and I did not mind.

Before I knew it, three months had gone by, and I had not been home. I really did not miss my community. I did miss seeing the family and the Swansons.

Anita was feeling well, and baby Eric had put on weight and had a great set of lungs. At dinner one night, I asked Lewis if he could help Anita with a few things like floors, clothes, and diapers. Maybe then, he could take me home instead of wasting his money paying me. He told me it was the best investment he'd made, hiring me, but it was time I went on with my life.

A few days later, they drove me to Kinnaird and tooted the horn on the car to get Ray's attention, to row across and get me. We also got the nasty ladies' attention as we got out of the car and said our sad farewells. Ray got my belongings into the boat, and I waved to the Burkes. Soon we were on the other side of the river, lined up on the bank near the ladies with scowls on their faces. I did not want to go there.

Ray said he would go ahead, and I stayed close behind.

They did not dare do or say anything at first. But halfway up the bank, the name-calling started, and then they said they saw the baby that I'd stayed away to have, giving it to those people. I was shocked and dismayed at such lies. Some things could not be explained to such ignorant people, so we did not try.

How was I going to live this down? Ray told them to go home, or he would call the police and have them thrown in jail for creating such malicious gossip and blasphemy. They got scared and ran, but I was more scared.

Ray said, "Hold your head up high, and do not speak to them or their friends. I know where you were. They are jealous of you because you speak English and they do not. They are ignorant and do not know anything about outside life."

Going home was not a happy time. I did not want to go to the Sunday meeting, but I did. I also did the ironing and pressing. Everyone at the Lordly's house was happy to see me, and they asked me assorted questions. All were curious about how I got along with everyone outside our community and how I was treated. I broke down and told them that people who did not live in the community treated me better than our own people did. I did nothing to deserve all this meanness. What was I supposed to do?

We lived by a beautiful river, tended beautiful gardens and orchards, and had some beautiful neighbors like the Landises and the Swansons. I met a lot of wonderful people all over the place, starting from Pelly and Yorkton to Saskatchewan, Brandon, Manitoba, Nelson, Trail, and Castlegar. Everyone was so nice and kind. Then I went home, and all our own people were so ignorant, mean, and jealous. I did not have anything they should be jealous about, and I was not unkind to anyone.

My little poem came to mind. "Oh, woe is me."

It was now summer. The gardens were planted, and I helped, but I kept my distance from all the gossip.

Things Could Be Better

One Sunday, Annie, Nellie, and I left Sunday meeting, in a big hurry to be away from all the mean gossip. We made a little detour, taking a different road that was a bit longer and rougher than the regular one. We ended up past a two-room schoolhouse. The children of Russian descent did not go there, but we were curious. The teacher was a beautiful lady, and she had a shiny blue dress and a kind voice. She asked us if we would like some lemonade, so we started talking to her. She asked all about me and told me she had heard of me and my sad experience. She asked if we wanted to come see her in the evenings occasionally, because she would teach us English.

Nellie backed out, but Annie and I promised her we would come every chance we got. We did go stealthily so no one would see us or hear of us going there. This gave Annie a chance to learn the language. I wanted my sister to learn to speak and read like me. This was another new venture for us.

One day someone called to me. I looked up, and a well-dressed gentleman was trying to converse with one of the ladies. She did not understand, and she had no choice but to call me over.

He said, "My name is Jeffery Watson. I am from Hadzic, a small place before you get to Vancouver. I have a lot of strawberries that need to be picked in four days' time. I will pay for eight ladies to come by train and work for me. I will pay wages and the return trip home. Can you get that many ladies to come and work for me?"

"We will have to get permission from Peter, the Lordly Verigin," I replied.

"Can we do it now?"

All the ladies nearby listened but did not understand.

I nodded my head yes and followed him to his car. A nice lady was sitting there, and she smiled as I got in. I said, "Hello, my name is Mary. I think I can help you."

With permission and the Lordly's blessings, I had seven ladies, including myself, interested in picking berries in Hadzic. The eighth one was my sister Annie; she had to see other parts of the province, and see there were other places and people.

My parents thought it was a ridiculous idea that the two of us were going, as did my sister Nellie. It was just as well I did not ask Nellie to come because she would not hear of it.

That evening, Annie got busy on our new sewing machine, which I'd bought with my last wages. She made us pants to wear when we were bending over to pick berries; that way no one could see our underpants.

We were packed the next day and ready to go. The other six ladies got so excited. Some laughed and some sobbed; they had never been away from their families before. They were in and out of our house with a million questions. Some of the girls sewed pants, and others just made panties because they'd never worn them before.

We all needed to pack blankets and a few changes of clothes. We also needed hats to shade our faces and heads. Mrs. Watson said she would provide hats for all of us, because they would get crushed in our packs.

In two days, we were ready to go. On the third day, some of the parents who had a horse and wagon took us to the station at Brilliant; the train stopped there regularly, because of the jam factory. We had tickets that the Watsons had bought for us, and we were excited. I should say most of the girls were excited; others were worried and scared. I tried to assure everyone that it would be all right.

Soon we were on the train and chugging away from the station. Then the important questions started. The girls wanted to know how to say hello and good-bye in English, as well as other everyday sayings. This was new and strange to them, so for hours they tried to ask and remember different things to say in English.

The train pulled into the station in Grand Forks. One of the girls recognized her cousin and waved and spoke to him. He looked worried about us, but I reassured him that all was going to be okay.

We were again on our way, and the conductor came through and brought everyone some water. Some of us had food from home, and we shared with those who did not have anything. Soon it was dark, and we tried to sleep. Morning came with bright sunshine coming through the windows and new scenery to see.

Eventually we came to flat green fields and farms with lots of cows, pigs in pens, chicken farms, and hay fields. It reminded some of the prairies that they'd left behind.

Soon the conductor announced the next stop would be Hadzic, where we would all get off the train. A farmer met us, and he said he was Mr. Watson Sr., but we should call him Joe.

We climbed into the back of a large truck; it had seats built across the back and down the sides. This truck was our transportation to and from the fields.

We had nice accommodations, one room with a stove, tables, and chairs, and a second room full of cots with mattresses. Outside was a washroom with cold and hot running water, and showers were set up in three separate cubicles. Outside were toilets. Everything was new and very clean, and the girls were told to keep it that way.

The next morning, as soon as the dew was off the strawberry plants, we rode on the back of the truck. Then we picked berries very carefully, so as not to squash any. The faster we picked, the more berries we would get, and the more we would be paid. We had a few breaks to go the outhouse, set at the edge of the field. We had pails of water and basins set out to wash our faces and hands. Then it was back to picking.

It was the first time for some of the girls. Most were used to bending over all day long because they had worked in the communal gardens. There were a few complaints, but most of the girls enjoyed being away from home.

At the end of the day, we were all tired, but most were happy. We washed up and enjoyed the showers once we got them working. We ate dinner and shared all the food we'd brought from home. We went to bed early for a few days.

When the day was done, as the girls got used to the work, during some evenings they sat around outside and had a happy, sing-song time. There was a lot of laughter, and all seemed to be very happy to share a new experience. We rose early, and no one needed to be told to get up.

This went on all week. Soon the berries were getting smaller, and there were fewer of them. Some of the ladies were asked to go to another farm to pick raspberries, and soon all of us went there.

After three weeks, we were told we could go home—unless some wanted to stay and work in the vegetable gardens. Most wanted to go home, so we all packed up.

The next day, we were on the train going home. Mr. Watson, or Joe as he wanted to be called, gave each of the girls a five-dollar bonus for doing such a good job, and he promised them a job next year if they came.

All the way home on the train, there was so much excitement about how the girls would spend their money. Then someone remembered they would have to turn it into the community funds, so they were silent after that. They wanted my opinion, but I did not know what to tell them.

Finally, I told them that I would speak to the Lordly and would get back to them. I did just that, and he suggested they give up half of their wages to the community, because others had done their work while they were away. With the other half, they should divide it in half again and give part to their parents. That would make it a quarter that they could keep for themselves. All were happy and satisfied with that arrangement; none had experienced this before.

I went home, got my share, gave a quarter of it to my parents, kept a quarter for myself, and took the rest to the Lordly. When I went to press his clothes the next day, he shook his head and said, "No. You keep this meager share. You taught the girls who went with you some responsibility. You have well earned it. It was not an easy job. You need this extra money for your medical needs and the bandages you insist on wearing."

I felt guilty and told him so. He said that I was not to mention this to anyone, and I did not. He also told me that in the following years as opportunities arose, I was to take other girls to do berry-picking jobs in other parts of the province, and he thanked me.

The seven girls were so pleased with being away and with the wages they got. It was a lot of money for people who'd had none before. They got me a beautiful shawl, a store-bought one. I thanked them from the bottom of my heart and meant it. I wore it to the sambranya (meeting) the following Sunday.

Some of our nasty neighbors were jealous. After the meeting, they followed me home and tormented me by giving me shoves, pulling on my new shawl, and calling me all kinds of cruel names. I ran as fast as I could until I could not run anymore.

Strict Reprimands

Four men were reprimanded after they got home from working in Niagara Falls. The parents had left for British Columbia before they returned, and so they came by train. They were supposed to hand in all their earnings to the community, but they'd bought clothes, suits, hats, shoes, and things for their parents and siblings. At Sunday's meeting, they were brought up in front of everyone, slapped around, and told they would no longer be part of the community if they did not turn in their money.

One of them, Misha Livko, gave to the community, and he was allowed to stay in Ootishenia. The other three would be dealt with at a later date.

On the way home, Nellie was walking with Wasya Edissov, making eyes at him and smiling. He walked her home and talked to Papa before he left.

That evening, I wanted to be filled in to what I had missed in the last three months.

Sister Annie had fallen in love with Ian, one of the men who came from Niagara Falls in a fancy suit and who smoked, and who was kicked out of the community. She said she was going to marry Ian. Papa did not know yet. She was determined to marry Ian regardless of what anyone said, and she would go with him wherever he went.

Nellie's friend Wasya had been married three times. He had a married daughter and son already, as well as three grandchildren, from the first two marriages. The wives had died, and he had a four-year-old son from the last marriage. That wife had died during childbirth, and the baby, a girl, had also died. He wanted Nellie to be his wife. She thought she loved him a bit. He and his family lived in Pass Creek.

The next morning, I gave Papa all the money I'd earned at the Burkes'. They also gave me a lot of clothes, sweaters, shoes, and dresses, and all the nasty ladies would frown at them if I wore them in the community, because they called them English clothes. I was happy to have them.

I went to Peter the Lordly's house with him. We were graciously received. Nastasia made us tea and brought out kolache. We gave the Lordly the money, and he said, "Do not give me this money, because you will be moving to Pass Creek in the near future. You will need this to fix up the living quarters."

He told us that he would get a team of horses and men to help us move. In the meantime, Papa would go to Pass Creek and look at the buildings to see what repairs were needed in order to make them livable for all of us.

The community built miles of stave water pipes, to provide water to the dry spots of Brilliant and Ootishenia. They piped water from Pass Creek after a dam was built to store water. The water was carried in stave pipes over a foot in diameter, on the bridge that was built across the Kootenay River and on to Ootishenia.

Sad Times

Peter the Lordly Verigin and his entourage were on their way to Grand Forks. He did not make it. Someone placed a bomb on the train and blew it up. It was a sad time for the Doukobour community and everyone who knew him.

There was a large funeral. The body was interred on a rock bluff overlooking the settlement of Brilliant and all the lands that he was instrumental in getting. Here he could forever oversee all the people who worked so hard. A monument was placed on the mountainside over his grave, and flowers were planted all around.

Now they were without a leader. It was a sad time for all.

Pass Creek

During this sad time, we nearly aborted our move to Pass Creek. The people in charge of the community told us it was not cancelled but put off for a while.

Papa still went there in his spare time, and he built a small house for my grandparents. There were other structures on the property. One building was a school, with two rooms added on for when the teacher lived there.

Grandpa did not make it to Pass Creek. He got pneumonia and died in his sleep. We were sad, and Grandma was devastated. We buried him in the cemetery just down the road, and she would go every day and cry at his graveside. We took turns getting her and bringing her home. It was so sad.

Meanwhile, Nellie got ready to marry Wasyl.

Papa built and repaired the existing buildings in Pass Creek, so that Nellie and Wasyl could use them.

We moved all our belongings one Sunday afternoon. We had a kitchen with a brick oven in which to bake bread. The Swansons gave us a stove, and Papa had made tables and chairs. He also made me a bed, and I had a bedroom of my own.

Nellie and Wasyl got married. We had a small

ceremony at our new home. The newlyweds had a small house of their own. Wasyl moved his and his sons' belongings into the new house Papa had built for them, and they were happy.

Soon Nellie was pregnant. She was so big with her baby that I got the new doctor to look at her. She was going to have twins! When she was in labor, I ran the seven miles to get the doctor. We came back in his car, and one of the babies had already been born. The two girls were so tiny that one did not make it; she took a few breaths and then died.

Nellie and Wasyl were so sad. They both doted on Annette, and they named the one who died Paulette and buried her at the local cemetery with a small service. I cried and cried. It should have been me, not her, because she was so loved.

However, I did not control things like that. I kept my chin up for everyone, and life went on. Through sad and happy times, I had to go on and try to help as much as I could. I'd help everyone amid all this sadness and not worry about myself.

Annie was madly in love with Ian. She told Papa, and he was sad, as was Mama. Ian came one evening to talk to our parents. He told them he loved Annie very much and would always look after her and any family they had. He begged my parents let them get married.

A few months later, they got married. They lived with Ian's parents, and they had a small bedroom, a kitchen, and a small living room, all nicely furnished. Ian even had a tap with water in the kitchen for her.

What joy for Annie and Ian. She was pregnant and announced it to us five months after they were married.

The coming October, Annie and Ian had the cutest little curly-haired boy. They called him Johnnie, and we were happy for them.

Happiness did not last too long for them.

New Beginnings

Three years had passed, and Peter the Lordly was replaced by Peter Chesticov, who came from Russia. He took over the Lordly's job, and the community helped him with unfinished business.

One of these unfinished businesses was the reprimand of the three men who had not handed over their money to the community. Ian, now my brother-in-law, was one of them. They worked hard for the community and handed in all their earnings, but it did not matter. They still had done wrong and had to pay, and they were made example of before the whole community.

The matter was dealt with one Sunday. Ian and two other men were called in front of the meeting and told that they could no longer live in the communal area. They could move to Rossland because there was a small parcel of land they could clear and farm; this was divided in three little sections, and they drew straws to see who got what section. It was not a happy time.

They were made fun of and laughed at by members of the community, but they held their heads up high and tried not to let it bother them. They had one week to get all their belongings together and move. They were able to use the community horses and wagon to do so, but then they were on their own.

We all helped Annie, Ian, and Johnnie, who was a year and half by then and was running around and talking. We were in tears. Rossland was not that far away, so we could go see them sometimes.

Soon after Annie, Ian, and Johnnie moved to Rossland, they told us they were going to have another baby. To make matters worse, Ian's brother tried to join the army. He was only sixteen years old, a year short of army age, and so Ian's father reported him to the local police. They caught up with him in Nelson. He did not want to get arrested or stopped from joining the army, so he locked himself in the bathroom at the rail train station and shot himself in the forehead. The bullet did not penetrate the skull bone, so he lived. He spent a week in the hospital and was sent back home.

On account of all this, the new leader, Chesticov, sent Ian's whole family to Rossland, where they settled next door to Ian, Annie, and Johnnie, as well as the new baby sister named after Ian's mother, Dora; they called her Dotty.

There they lived for four years. They wanted to be independent of the Doukobour community, but this was still community property.

Ian worked in the forest for an American gentleman. He logged in the forest with a team of horses. He worked in Blueberry Creek. Mr. Lowe told him there was a house to rent there, so why not move? The whole family moved, and Ian's parents and siblings moved to a rental house just up the hill. They were closer to us again.

The house where Peter Lordly had lived in the Waterloo area was still occupied by Nastasia, and I would occasionally go do her clothes for her.

Every Sunday I would walk to the Chesticov house, which was built in Brilliant. I would still do the pressing OR the ironing of their clothes. I would rise early, walk seven miles, attend the morning meeting, and then go do my work.

Brilliant now had a train station, the Brilliant Jam factory, a grain elevator, and a flourmill. The area grew fruit and vegetables, shipping a lot to the prairie and provinces by train.

The Slocan Valley had logging and manufactured bricks. The area was flourishing.

Pass Creek

At home we all worked hard. In the spring, Papa and Nellie's husband would plow the garden plots. We would seed assorted vegetables, like potatoes, carrots, beets, turnips, and cabbage that would keep in the winter months in root cellars. We would can a lot of fruit and berries, making lots of jams and jellies. We also pickled many things, like melons, cabbage, and even apples. All this was stored for the winter months.

Things like salt, flour, and sugar had to be bought. Papa and Wasya worked in the forestry trade, with logging or sawmills. Many men made a living making bricks. Part of their wages still went to the community, as did my wage.

Occasionally someone from Trail or Nelson would come get me to do housework. I came highly recommended by the people for whom I had previous worked. They ignored the fact that I had a bandage on my nose, and I did a lot of different jobs. With that money, I would provide the extra essentials that our family needed.

Soon we had a couple of cows, a horse, and chickens. When the hens sat, we had baby chicks. Someone even gave us a goat. Nana was a brat, and when one called her, she would *baa* as if talking back to you.

Nellie had a new baby, a boy named Michael, and so little Annette had a brother. She worshipped her older stepbrother, Alosha. He was such a kind and obedient child, and we all loved him.

Come springtime, the fruit farmers would recruit pickers. Later, a lot of them came to me because I had a reputation of knowing supply girls who would work and do a thorough job.

Many times I would be very lonely, especially when I would get a note from Brandon, from Ern. He was now a doctor, like his father. He was married to a lovely girl, and I was happy for him. I would send him a brief note—very brief, because I was forgetting my English writing.

I still kept in contact with my friends in Trail, and I also made new ones. I worked any chance I got, and I would walk to Castlegar and then catch a train to Trail. It worked out for me, and I got to wear my English clothes more often.

The people were more understanding where we now lived. They were more independent of the community living, even if they went to meetings and prayer times in Brilliant. Some owned their own vehicles, and often they would give me a ride to or from Castlegar.

Most times I walked. It was something I did well. I would walk across the Columbia River on the railway bridge, up to Pass Creek Road and home. I knew a few shortcuts if it was early in the day.

One day, Les Mokowsky caught up with me. He introduced himself and told me he wanted to walk with me. I saw no harm in that. Many times he would walk me as far as the road, bid me good-bye, and turn around and go back to Castlegar. I got used to him doing this, and one day I asked why was he doing this.

"Because I think I am falling in love with you," he replied with a big grin. That was impossible, but he did sound very sure of himself.

That was when I panicked. It was something I did not expect. "Why would you love me?" I did not encourage him, but I did not discourage him. I thought, *This cannot go on any longer. I have to put a stop to this.* I told him that I did not even like him. I could be a friend, but nothing else. We remained friends for a long time.

I did not see him for a long time. Then one day, he appeared again. He told me, "I am ready to get married. Will you marry me?"

I was petrified, "No, I cannot marry you. I do not love you enough to marry you, and you cannot love me enough to marry me."

He tried to assure me that he did love me.

I broke it off because I was too scared. I was not the marrying kind. I expected to be a spinster my whole life.

I learned a few months later that Les married a girl from Trail. He was such a nice guy, and I was sure they would be happy. I thought, *Could I have been happy with him? And could he have been happy with me? We will never know.*

Scary Experience

One evening I was walking home. It was late fall and getting cold. Andrew Samolo stopped his logging truck to give me a ride. When I got in, I realized he had been drinking. Everyone know he drank too much. I was scared of him. Why did I get in, even if I was six miles away from home? He started talking nasty to me, asking if I was a virgin and whether he could fix that. He pulled off the road at a wider area. As he reached for my leg, I opened the door and bolted.

I ran back along the road, knowing he could not turn the truck around fast. He was right behind me, huffing and puffing. I ran up a narrow pathway, not knowing where it led, and hid in the bushes.

I was so scared that I was shaking. I then realized I had left my small, embroidered purse, as well as the two bags of groceries, in the truck. I could hear Andrew calling and saying he was sorry, and to please come back; he would not hurt me. He asked me not to tell anyone, especially his wife. He sounded like he was sorry. But there was no way could I trust him, drunk or sober.

Soon I heard the truck start and drive away.

I waited to make sure he was gone, and then I went

back to the road. I ran most of the way home. I ducked off the road every time a vehicle came.

Everyone was in bed except Nellie. I told her what happened. Nellie must have told Wasya; he got up the next morning and was gone when the rest of us got up.

We were having breakfast when a truck pulled up to the gate. Wasyl got out, followed by Andrew, who was disheveled and upset looking, but carrying my bags; he had put my purse into one of the grocery bags. He would not come inside but wanted a word with me.

I went out and stood looking scornfully at him. He looked worried and had tears in his eyes. He said he was sorry; he'd never done anything so stupid in his life. It must have been the liquor he'd had, because he had never done that to anyone. "Would you please, not tell anyone, and please forgive me?" he begged. I could catch a ride with him anytime and never worry again—Wasyl had threatened him with his life.

Wasyl and I told everyone the bags were too heavy to carry, so Andrew had driven them home for me. Nellie, Wasyl, and I kept quiet. I think Andrew even quit drinking for a while. His wife told Mama when she met her that he was a better man to live with, and the children were no longer afraid of him.

I guessed some good could come out of bad things sometimes.

Summer's Picking

In May, a man came from Creston area, known for growing strawberries, raspberries, and cherries. He said to me, "I understand you speak some English, and you can get me some pickers to pick berries. Later on, I will give you some money for the train ride to Creston, for seven ambitious young ladies. You will be in charge, and they will do as you tell them, because I do not speak Russian. Do you think you can do this? I will provide living quarters for them."

"I certainly can get ladies who can pick berries and would love to work for you," I replied. We settled on the date we would take the train.

I got a few girls from our area, and then I walked to Krestovea, a Sons of Freedom settlement. My grandpa's sister's family lived there, as did Papa's sister. I had no trouble convincing three more girls from there to come pick berries. I set stipulations. There was to be no fighting between regular Doukobours and the other group, and no discussing differences of religions. They would all get along, or I personally would send them home.

The day came to go to Creston. All the girls were at the Castlegar train station, their gunnysacks packed with blankets, pillows, extra clothes, and personal stuff. Everyone had a box filled with canned jars of food, bread, and lapsh (noodles). They were chattering merrily, happy to be going on a new adventure.

We were picked up by Mr. Wolfgang and piled into the back of the truck. He took us down a dusty road to his place. There was a little house, and it had three bedrooms, beds with mattresses, a few cupboards, and some drawers. We drew straws to see who got which ones. There was one kitchen with a cook stove, table and chairs, and assorted dishes, which we all shared.

Everything went peacefully and friendly, and I was happy about that.

The next day was the start of picking. Many had picked before, and those who were new were introduced to how it was done. It went smoothly.

A local boy named Malcomb collected our berries and punched our cards. He took a liking to Nataska, a cute blonde girl, and would smile at her every time he went by.

I was very irate at the end of the day, when I took a good look at my punched berry card. I had nowhere near enough punches on my card. I checked the girls' cards, and Natashka had the most, though I knew she did not pick that much. I saw Mr. Wolfgang, and we had a discussion and got my card punched properly.

The next day Malcomb was there, cheery as ever. Mr. Wolfgang was also around all morning, checking very closely. Pretty soon Malcamb was called aside by the boss, and he also called Natashka and me over. We quickly got things straightened out, and there were no more "mistakes." After that, all went well. Malcomb did not even say he was sorry. He was quite arrogant.

One evening Mr. Wolfgang treated the girls to a train ride into Creston and a movie show with popcorn, as well as drinks and ice cream cones on the return trip. How exciting! This was the first movie for all of them, so they were happy.

Happy girls made happy workers. In the evenings, they sat around. Some knitted, some embroidered, and some crocheted, but most just chatted. All were having a great time. They sang many happy songs. They thanked me constantly and wanted to come back the next year.

They talked about how they were going to spend their earnings. It was not much, but it was more than they had seen before. The last day, we went to Creston after we got paid. Most of the girls bought sweaters. They wore these and no one criticized them.

It was time to go home, and the girls were sad. All stayed friends—Sons of Freedom and Orthodox Doukobours. They were simply people, and it did not matter what they believed in. Religions do not matter; be you a Catholic or Protestant or Baptist. There are nice people everywhere. To me, nationality, color, and religion does not matter; it is who you are inside. It is how you treat other people that counts. Everyone has to be treated equally in my world, and then it will be a better place in which to live.

As Life Goes On

My parents were happy to see me. I gave a quarter of my earnings to them, kept a quarter for my expenses, and took the rest to the community cause. They gave me back half of it again. I still did my ironing duties, and everyone was happy to see me and have nicely pressed clothes again. That counted as my payment to the community.

I visited my Trail friends and got a few jobs for the fall.

I helped Annie and Ian with their move to Kinnaird. They had a big house. We stripped all the wallpaper off the walls, replaced it with clean new paper, and painted the wood on some of the walls, doors, and all the trim. It was like a new house. There was a shed, barn, hay shed, and a few smaller out buildings, situated by the river overlooking Ootishenia, where we'd lived before. Water was pumped into a reservoir, then into the kitchen sink.

Ian built a banya, a bathhouse, out of one of the smaller buildings. Annie did the laundry there, and the children bathed there. They were getting grown up and going to school. Ian still had his logging, and now he had two horses. Papa gave him a cow, and I walked her from Pass Creek. I had to cover her eyes with my sweater because she would not go onto the ferry, but we made it to Kinnaird and her new home with no further trouble.

The next morning, Ian went to see the cow, and there was a new baby there. We thought the cow was just fat, but she had a female calf. It was a two-in-one gift for their new place!

Johnnie and Dotty were growing like weeds. They were well-behaved children. Annie bleached and dyed flour sacks assorted colors and made them into clothes. She embroidered on Dotty's dresses and knit sweaters and socks for the children and Ian. She knit Ian heavy socks to wear in the forest; these kept him dry and warm in the winter months. The children had new clothes as they went up the hill to catch the school bus to Castlegar.

Annie also knitted socks and sweaters, to send to the soldiers who were fighting in the war in Europe. The Doukobour community was sending assorted jams from the Brilliant jam factory—cases and cases of all flavors. The ladies were making socks and sweaters for soldiers to keep them warm, because it was winter there.

Annie and Ian still had friends across the river. They had a wooden boat made by their friend Petro, so they would row across the river and visit with old friends while I babysat the children. The children were good, and we played little games. I enjoyed them.

I would visit and help for a few days, and then I'd catch the train to Castlegar, purchase a few groceries and necessities, and walk home.

Occasionally Andrew's large truck would lumber up, and he would offer me a ride. My answer was always no. Then he would offer to take my groceries home for me.

He apologized every time and told me he no longer drank and took good care of his family. He was so embarrassed. I still did not trust him.

In the winter, I worked for a lady who owned a department store in Castlegar. I would clean her house because she had no family. It was very clean all the time, and she paid me well. I spent some of the money in her store on things like shoes for my family, as well as other necessities.

Peter Verigin (Chesticov) moved to his new house in Brilliant. I still went every Sunday and did the ironing for him, making sure all was neatly pressed and hung up in the new wardrobes.

John Verigin came from Russia to live with the Doukobours. I made sure all his clothes were neat and clean too. He was a nice, young, and gentle person, and he was very kind to me. He went to school and made many friends. The Doukobours were told they were supposed to go to school; that was the law. All the children were happy to do so. They would learn to read and write, and many went on to be lawyers and teachers. Times changed, and they went to school—unlike me. I had had to sneak out in order learn to read and write from the kindly Miss Simmons.

It was not like the Sons of Freedom's children. Their parents would not let them go to school, so the government officials came to their homes and took the crying and scared children away to be educated elsewhere. Papa's sister's children were sent to Vancouver. The sister, my aunt, came to the house with a letter for me to read and translate. It was from one of her daughters, who was loving it in Vancouver and enjoying learning. She said that most of the children were happy to be learning new things, and we should tell their parents they were doing all right.

My aunt cried but was happy to realize the children were being looked after, and all was well.

I Do Not Like Goats

One fall day, as I was walking home, I went past John and Masha's little farm. I noticed the gate was opened. It was never opened, because that was where the billy goat was penned in—but he was not there. All at once, I heard *thump, thump* behind me. before I could turn around, I was bumped on my behind and sent flying on my stomach, face-first into the gravel on the road. The billy goat was loose and after me.

"Help! John, Masha, help!" I yelled.

The goat backed up, and with his head down, all I could see were his ears and large horns. I do not remember how I got to my feet and up on to the wooden fence, but I made it, still screaming for help.

John came running from the house. He had a big stick and was swinging at the goat, who was butting the fence just below me. Soon he had him back in the corral. I was still shaking and hurt and dirty. My hands were bleeding, and my groceries were scattered all over the road. Masha came to help. We picked up the stuff, and she insisted I go into the house and get cleaned up.

After washing up, taking care of my wounds, and picking out gravel from my knees and hands, I used the extra bandages in my bag. They came in handy. John and Masha hovered over me and were so worried. Soon I left because I still had five miles to walk. After that, I was pretty cautious about walking past their place. I hated goats.

Relatives

We had many relatives still living in Saskatchewan. Papa's sister Dasha and her husband came to visit almost every year. They brought us freshly ground flour, cranberries, freshly killed geese, and some beef. They came in October, so the meat stayed fresh because it was cold. We did not eat meat, so the geese and beef were for Ian's parents; they still ate meat and were no longer living in the Doukobour community.

Another sister of Papa's lived in Pelly, but she occasionally came to visit. They stayed on a farm and raised cattle. They did exceptionally well.

An aunt of Papa's lived in Krestova. Her husband was a member of Sons of Freedom, the breakaway sect of the Doukobours. Papa would not have anything to do with them, and we were told not to associate with them.

I did get girls from Krestova to pick berries, and they were happy to go and get a few dollars of their own. One of them was a cousin, Papa's niece.

One Sunday during a celebration in Brilliant the Orthodox Doukobours had, the Sons of Freedom group came. They were not invited and not wanted, and they disrupted the meeting. They started to undress and protest in their own way. Some of the young girls were undressing, much to our chagrin. It was so sad that they were brought up to do this. I think the old men were enjoying this, which was sad. I recognized one of the girls as my aunt's daughter, Papa's niece. I was very angry, snatched up her clothes, grabbed her by the arm, and dragged her out of the crowd. All the Sons of Freedom were screaming at me. I got her behind some bushes and made her put on her clothes. She was shaking and sobbing, but she listened to me and got dressed.

The rest of the nudes were now singing and preaching. I guessed I was on their bad list because one of them was yelling at me, adding that they would burn down our house. They yelled that they would undress me the first chance they got. I told them I would have the police put them in jail if they did anything to me, my family, or my friends.

I was scared, and for months we guarded our property. Papa was given a big collie by the Landises. He would bark to announce if someone came, but he was very friendly. He was not Koodrick from Russia, but he was beautiful. We called him Laddie, and Papa called him Lad. Lad followed Papa everywhere, and he would meet me at the gate.

Sometimes I would bring him a bone from town.

He was happy, very obedient, and smart. He was a real guard dog.

Even so, after the ordeal, we did not sleep well for many nights.

Life as Usual

As summer wore on and fall came, we dug up the carrots, beets, and potatoes and stored everything in the root cellar. Papa and Wasya had made the cellar into the hillside and covered it with dirt to make it cooler in the summer and warmer for the winter. We stored cabbages and turnips too. We had received a few boxes of winter pears and apples, and these were tasty treats in the long winter months.

We had many friends come and visit. No one left hungry, or at least they had a cup of tea and Mama's famous biscuits (kolache) with honey. Papa was given a hive of bees, so we ended up with honey for the cold winter months. We were becoming well-known for our kolache and honey. A lot of our friends started calling us Kalachovi, instead of our regular name.

Papa made a long shed for the hives, as well as a few extra hives in anticipation of having more hives next spring. When he checked the one hive, he found an extra queen bee, which the bees were nurturing. We ended up with extra bee hives.

Papa kept busy during the winter months. He built a banya with a rock sauna, and it was wonderful. He also built a workshop, where he carved spoons. He would sand them so thin that the light could almost be seen though them. He also made wooden bowls, cutting boards, spinning wheels, wool carders, and spools for the spinning wheels.

One day he asked me if I liked the color maroon. A few days later, I was told to get Papa from his carpentry shop. When I went to get him, I noticed the whole family was right behind me. Papa presented me with a maroon spinning wheel all my own, a bit smaller than everybody else's. I put my arms around him and cried, thanking him over and over again. It was beautiful, and it was all mine. What a pleasant surprise. He had taken time to build this for me, when he could have been doing something else.

Everyone hugged me as I wiped tears from my eyes. I was so lucky to be blessed with such a great family.

Papa carved spoons, and he told me I could take some to my friends in Nelson and Trail, to give them away as gifts. These were greatly appreciated by all my friends.

Summers Picking Fruit

Every summer I would get girls together, and we picked strawberries and raspberries in the Creston area. Then when they were finished, we would regroup and go to the Okanagan areas to pick cherries, apricots, peaches, pears, and apples.

We needed a few strong men to move the ladders for us. A couple of the ladies got their husbands to come, because some were unemployed. They thanked me for the opportunity to earn a few dollars, which were shared with the community when they returned home.

As Days Go By

I led a very sheltered, boring life—or so I thought. I guess it was not any more boring than a lot of other people had.

One fall I decided to go back to Saskatchewan to visit Papa's sister and her family. I wrote to her, and she cordially replied that they would love to have me visit.

I packed my English clothes, my dresses and a nice wool suit, as well as a few gifts for everyone: a box of pears, some plums, and three boxes of apples. Papa put me on the train the next day. I smiled and was happy to be going.

What a gossip session I created! Some said I was going to Brandon to see my boyfriend. (I wished.) Some said my nose was infected, and some said I was pregnant. Those people were not my friends, as I'd long ago figured out. Let them talk. I told my family to ignore it all. I realized these people did not have much of a life, and if I added some excitement to it, so be it.

Soon I was on my way. I saw Nelson, Creston, and other familiar places I had seen on my trip to Brilliant from Brandon. Places had changed, and new towns were made with train stops.

I saw a lot of new buildings being built. Places like

Kimberly, Natal, and Michell were coal mining and smelting places. Some were sort of black like Trail, from coal and smelters. It was very interesting how time changed places. But I was still the same. I did not believe I'd changed at all.

As the train chugged along and the wheels clanged, I remembered all that had happened to me over the years. Some memories were good and some bad, some happy times and some sad. I remembered the people I'd met in my lifetime. Some were good people, but some were not so good; some were kind, and some were mean.

Most of the time, I tried to forget the bad ones and remember the good ones. I realized there were more good people than bad ones on the earth. Or maybe I chose to remember only the good, and the bad were not worth remembering. At least, that was how I felt.

I still wore a bandage on my nose. Yes, I knew it had healed a long time ago. However, I did not want people to stare at my nose—or no-nose, as some nasties would say to me. People still stared at the bandages. The train chugged and tooted, and sometimes it stopped at small towns that had sprouted up from the bald prairies. I was very relaxed to be on my own again, and I was tired too. Occasionally I would snooze.

The journey went by quickly because I enjoyed this trip. The three days came to an end. The conductor called out, "Yorkton, next stop—the end of the line."

My cousin Dasha's husband, Soma, was at the station to meet me. I expected to see a team of horses. Instead, I saw a bright, shiny new black car. I noticed the nice, clean smell as I got in the front seat next to Soma. He filled me in on what had happened in Kamsack, Saskatchewan. His store was very successful, and he made a great deal of money. He made the store larger, and his boys, Sam and Mike, worked there on weekends and after school.

I was very happy for them. I was welcomed with open arms by Dasha and their boys. The baby was a tiny little one and started to cry; she was only a year old and was cute. Dasha and Soma said she looked a lot like me when I was little.

I stayed at their place for a whole month, helped in the store, and looked after the baby. I also ran into some of our neighbors from the time we'd lived in Pelly. Some wanted to visit, and some were simply nosy. I handled the meetings well. Some stayed in Saskatchewan and did well as farmers; the farmers flourished and bought more land, horses, and new machinery to make the work easier.

Some were nosy, and they had questions about my previous boyfriend. They asked if I'd seen him and his wife, because they lived in Ootshenia, where we had lived. I answered them as simply and politely as I could.

Of course I did see him, and I knew he had children, three girls. I was not envious or jealous, as some people seemed to think. I wished them the best of everything, and happiness forever.

I also went to the other cousin's house. She had just wed the love of her life, her third one, so I did not want to be in their way. I did not stay long, only a few days. They introduced me to their neighbor, who was a Polish gentleman. He was very polite, hard working, and kind, and he was a successful farmer.

He told me he was looking for a wife. Two days later,

he came to propose to me. Of course I said no. He did not understand why I did not want to marry him. He had land, he had a nice house, and he had some money that he was willing to share. He said he would take good care of me.

I was so afraid I was not good enough for him. He could not understand why I thought this. I could not marry him. I did not love him—I did not even like him. He said we could learn to love each other. I could not saddle him with my ugly face. He said he did not look at it that way. I thanked him and said good-bye.

Was I being stupid? My cousin tried to talk some sense into me. I was afraid, and I ran away from real life. I had to face my feelings about myself. He did not see things realistically. Until I learned to like me, I could not like or love anyone else.

A few days later, I got on the train and went back home.

I thought all the way home, *Could I have been happy? Could I have made him happy?*

I decided that I had done the right thing. There was no sense in making someone else unhappy and burdened with my unhappiness. I did not want some man to look at my face and think he could have done better than me. Even I did not like me.

I went back home, to my own misery. The trip home was uneventful.

Kinnaird

I did not get off the train in Castlegar. Instead, I went on to see Annie and her family in Kinnaird. Ian was in the woods, logging with his two new horses. Annie was home looking after Johnnie and Dotty.

Nicholas and Dora, the in-laws, were there visiting Annie and the children. They told me their latest news about Lorne, their son, who'd joined the army too young. Lorne had to report to the police every week. He was doing well and was engaged to marry Tina, a girl he'd known most of his life.

Johnnie was now in grade two, and Dotty had started grade one. They sat there and tried their English on me. Soon we had a real conversation going, and the grandparents joined in. Nicholas spoke a great deal, and the children were thrilled to hear him speak the English language.

We spent a wonderful evening reminiscing about our trip to Canada, and all that had happened since then. They were not unhappy about leaving the Doukobour community and living in Blueberry Creek. They had made many friends.

Then they told us about Mary, their daughter, Ian's

sister. We knew she'd had a son out of wedlock and sued Eli Stovow for support. He got a bunch of buddies to say they all had a relationship with her. She left the area and went to Vancouver, had a son (Billie), and was coming back home the following week with her new husband, Nickie Smart.

Of course Fred, their youngest son, wanted to marry his longtime girlfriend, Mable Pozdnikowa. They did not like her and were much against her. He called off the marriage and said he was going to Vancouver with Mary and Nickie when they got back.

We had a nice visit with Annie's in-laws.

Annie announced that after seven years, she was pregnant again. We were happy, but she was worried.

In the morning, I went back to Pass Creek and my parents, and to Nellie and her family. Alex, her stepson, was in grade six this fall; Annette was in grade two. They both loved school. Michael could hardly wait to start school next year.

I spent most of the winter working for Larrissa. Our cousin on our mom's side of the family had left her womanizing husband and married Larrissa's brother George, who adopted her two sons. They lived in a large house in Nelson.

Not Too Much Change

Life went on, and not too much changed. Annie was pregnant, and she had a rough pregnancy, so I spent a lot of time with her. She was sick for quite a while, and I was with her when the baby was due. Ian was working at the time.

She went into labor. Our cousin was also there. The baby was so stubborn in coming that cousin Aylla told me to go to Castlegar and get Dr. Gaeyton right away.

"Run all the way," were her words.

Good things did happen. The doctor was in his office, and he got his black bag and told me to get in the car. He made good time in getting to Kinnaird. I got out to open the gates, and he told me to leave the gates open. He did not waste time. He gave a look and feel of Annie's stomach, and he said the baby was coming breech, feet first.

We got her in the car and left Aylla, our cousin, to look after the other two children when they got home from school. We drove to Trail Hospital. Annie was so worried about what Ian would say about her going into the hospital. The doctor was not worried about that.

We got to the hospital in no time at all. I was

impressed that cars could go so fast. I tried to keep Annie comfortable, but she was in terrible pain. I went into the delivery room with her, and she was so exhausted that she was barely breathing. The doctor put her on oxygen, and after a great deal of pushing on Annie's part, and twisting and pulling on the doctor's part, the baby arrived not breathing. I was worried, and the nurses were frantic as they held the baby. The doctor cleared the baby's nose and mouth. He then held the baby upside down and gave it a whack on the behind.

Out of the baby's little mouth came a loud howl. The baby cried and was all right. Then we found out the little one was a girl. She weighed a bit over six pounds and had a loud cry. Annie was sedated because she was exhausted, and she said she hoped she would never have another baby.

Annie and Ian had the baby eight years after Dotty. The cute, blue-eyed girl was named Velda. Then two years later, they had a boy, Peter. All were healthy and happy. Dotty and Johnnie were eight and ten years old, respectively, and did not want a new baby in the house. But after getting used to the new sister and brother, they were quite happy to have the other two in the family.

Velda tagged along after the older two, even when they did not want her along. She was their chatty little sister and could talk her way into everything. She had cute blonde hair and blue eyes. The others had dark hair, and the boy's hair was curly.

Back to Annie's in-laws. Their daughter, Mary, left her son, Billie, with her parents, Nicholas and Dora. Fred, her brother, and a cousin named Gerald left with her and her husband, Nickie, when they went to Vancouver. But first Fred and Mary knew that Dora hid their money in balls of wool yarn that she used to make socks. The brother and sister cut the yarn balls and took their life savings. Nicholas was very angry, as was Ian; he'd told them to place their savings in a bank in Castlegar, and they had not.

Life Is So Short

Billie loved his grandparents, who were doting on him and treating him well. He missed his mother. Instead of going to the grandparents' home, he came to Ian and Annie's, and he called them Mama and Papa. Annie sewed him pants and shirts, as she did for her own children. She treated him like he belonged to them.

Mary did not come back for him. She did come back, but to a sadder time.

During the next summer holidays, when he was twelve years old, he went swimming in Blueberry Creek. He got caught in the rapids and drowned. His friends tried to save him, but the river ran too swiftly. The police rescue team found his body a short distance downstream from the rapids.

This was a sad time for all. Billie was gone. He had endeared himself to many people, and it was a big funeral. He was buried in Ootishenia Cemetery.

Mary came back for the funeral loaded down with gifts for Ian and Annie's children. She had cute dresses for Velda and new shoes. Mary tried to impress Velda with the new puppy she had. Then she took Velda in her and Nickie's car, and she tried to talk Annie and Ian into letting her have Velda. They had four children, and she had none, so she could take one her back to Vancouver.

Ian told her he did not want to see her anywhere near any of his children. If she had looked after Billie, there may not have been a funeral that day. Of course the answer was no.

That night, Ian got a friend to drive me and Velda to Pass Creek, so she was in my care until Mary left for Vancouver.

As time went on, Johnnie, Dotty, and the younger two spent a lot of time with us. We loved them, and they loved us. They got along with Nellie's children. They also made friends with a lot of the neighbors' children.

Life continued as usual. I still walked to Brilliant and did my ironing and cleaning. I got along with everyone there. The new residence was very nice. John was very nice, had lots of friends, and did well in school. Some Sundays when he was home, he would drive me home to Pass Creek. It was almost like he knew when I was tired, and I certainly appreciated the ride.

On the farm, we had chickens, horses, cows, and a large garden. We did well. I still took odd jobs. Annie and Ian got me some jobs with the new Kinnaird settlers. A lot of houses were being built in Kinnaird and Castlegar.

The children were growing up. My favorite was little Velda, who was a tiny, wiry, and outgoing child. If she got something in her mind, she would do it.

Ian's mother, Dora, got hit by a car and spent time convalescing with Annie, because Ian was working. Nicholas was so sad. Then to make matters worse, Dora had a stroke, and her left side was paralyzed.

Nicholas and Dora moved in with Annie and Ian. There were four bedrooms in the house. Dora spent some time in a large entrance made into a bedroom for her. We fixed up a larger bedroom for Nicholas and her upstairs; when she got better, she was able to walk upstairs. She had to learn to walk, but her vocal cords did not improve beyond one-syllable words; it was hard for her. They thought it was terrific that they did not have to walk up the mountain to their place in Blueberry Creek.

Little Dotty and Johnnie each had a bedroom up there too.

I spent as much time as I could there, and I slept on the couch in the living room. I helped Annie with the kids and in-laws. Ian worked hard, and when he came home from the woods job, he still had to bring in hay for winter and wood for the stoves. All the garden produce had to be stored in a root cellar. I tried to help.

Often I would take the younger children home with me.

Life continued without much interesting going on.

The children had all grown up. Soon even Velda and Peter were in school and could not visit us often.

Annette got married to Mike Kanihin.

Alex was away working, and then he came home and got a local school custodian's job, to be closer to our aging parents.

Johnnie got a construction job on the highway, in the Princeton, Hedley, and Hope areas.

Ian was home and worked on the Brilliant power dam. He rode his bike to work after rowing the boat across the river.

Little Dotty met John and fell in love. He was seven years older, and she had turned sixteen. Come January, they got married.

Sad Times

In 1946, Nicholas sat outside and enjoyed the balmy summer evening in July. He told Velda and Peter his usual stories about the olden days. All at once, he fell over in his chair. Peter ran to get Annie from the garden, and she sent Velda running to Castlegar, to fetch Dr. Gorkey. They got back as quickly as they could.

In the meantime, Annie, with a little help from Dora, got Nicholas on a cot in the living room. She washed him and made him as comfortable as possible. He was unresponsive.

Grandma Dora was holding his hand and weeping. Annie was in shock, wringing her hands and also sobbing. When Johnnie came home, he was sent to Waneta Logging Camp to tell his dad about Grandpa.

Weeping was what Dr. Gorkey found in the house. After checking Nicholas's vitals, he informed them of the stroke. There was nothing he could do, and he would not move Nicholas to a hospital. If Nicholas were to awaken and become aware of his surroundings in a few days, he would be okay—or he may pass away in his sleep. Only time would tell.

Six days later, Nicholas passed away, having never

regained consciousness. He was buried in Ootishenia Cemetery a few rows from his grandson Billie. The cemetery was across the Columbia River, from where he had rowed many times to see his friends, and down the road from where he had lived many years ago.

Castlegar Is Growing, and so Is Kinnaird

The owner of the Kinnaird property that Ian and Annie had rented all these years decided to subdivide it into lots and sell the property. He offered Ian the bottom part by the river: four acres or so, but no water or power. Three thousand dollars was a lot of money, and Ian did not have it. They wanted a little farm with cows, horses, and chickens. A little garden was a must.

Ian's uncle, Paul, loaned him money for a ten-acre farm in the Slocan Valley.

During the Easter school holiday in 1947, Ian loaded a friend's large truck twice, and they took all their belongings to Slocan Park. Then came moving day. Dotty and her new husband, John, loaded the station wagon with Grandma Dora, Mom, Peter, Velda and the black-and-white cat Pearl.

The trip was not without a few outbursts from Velda. She did not want to go. She went back into the house and got a little bag from behind the attic stairs, her favorite hiding place. She was not taking things she hated. The bag contained barrettes, suspenders, a coloring book she thought was boyish, stockings she did not think fashionable, and other things she was given and did not like. They lay hidden under the third step for years, for no one to see.

She had to move. She said good-bye to all her old friends at school and at home. She and Peter said good-bye to all their favorite spots in the 295 acres they called home. They said good-bye to all their friends, including Mr. and Mrs. Heinzes and their two black cats, whom they befriended when they delivered fresh milk every morning before getting on the bus to school.

This was what she confided in me, after making me swear to never tell anyone. She said she would never come to visit me if I told anyone.

The next time I saw them all was when I went to visit their new home.

Getting Older

As years went on, I did not seem to get old. Everyone around me was old. A great deal of my friends got old and sick and even passed away. I babysat their children's children. I still went with some friends who did not learn English, translating where necessary. Some were appreciative, and some figured I owed it to them.

Mama got sick and passed away. I was very sad, and we all missed her.

Alosha was now driving a nice Dodge car. He got Annie's family and brought them to the funeral. Dotty and John came, as did Johnnie; he now worked on the construction of the Alaska highway.

Nellie's Wasyl died after that.

Grandma Dora died shortly after. That generation was going.

The next year, Papa died. I was so sad.

The New Generation

Soon I was blessed with great-nieces and great-nephews. Annette and Mike had a girl. Dotty and John had a girl, two months younger than Annette's baby.

A year and a half later, Annette had a boy. They lived close to us.

Dotty and John built a new home that was also close.

Peter, Annie, and Ian's youngest went to work with Johnnie on the West Coast. He was too young, and we worried because Johnnie sent him to work on the north end of the island. But he came back to Vancouver and got a job building the tunnel on Dease Island for a nice boss, who insisted he go back to school. He did so at nights and graduated.

Velda was seeing Pedro and was engaged. She was over to see us. She worked Alex's custodian job when he went to the hospital to get his appendix removed. She and Nellie did not get along well. Nellie made her wear woolen stockings to keep her feet warm; she got a rash from them. Nellie got shingles. Both were aching when we got home from Nelson, and they were glad to see me.

Velda got married in August. It was a nice wedding, but the groom's family was not sociable. She was not happy, she told me. Pretty soon she was also pregnant. They moved to Castlegar, and she was happier there. She had the baby girl, Dasha, in Trail Hospital.

I gave all my nieces and nephews some money to help buy lots in Kinnaird, or to put toward building there.

Velda and her family built across the street from Dotty's family.

On my next birthday, I turned seventy years old. Velda had a party for me in their unfinished house. All the nieces and nephews, my sisters, and Ian were there. What a pleasant surprise! We had a cake with seventy candles; I thought the house would catch fire. They had a money tree for me, and they found out I was going back to Saskatchewan with Ian's uncle and his new wife that fall. It was the best June 14 I'd had in my seventy years, and I cried and laughed.

The family was building a house and living in it while they worked. They asked me to spend my winters there and fixed an extra room for me. It was better than carrying wood and water, and freezing in Pass Creek. My residence was old and cold with no running water. I promised them I would next winter.

In the meantime, I would go and enjoy my trip. Everyone was happy for me, and wished me a safe and happy journey.

A Trip Not So Enjoyable

Paul picked me up in Pass Creek. My suitcase was all packed, and I said my good-byes to Nellie, Michael, and Alex. Our new dog and cat sat by the car and watched, and I gave them a rub on their heads.

With Paul in the car was Helen, his new wife, and Marisha Volkin. We were picking up Erina Osacha in Kinnaird. Soon we were on our way, all chatty and happy.

We wished Paul and Helen a happy time together and the very best of everything.

We went to Balfour across Kootenay Lake, over to Creston. We had a coffee stop in Cranbrook and were cheerful, having a good time. Soon enough, we were in the town of Crows Nest and moved on into Alberta. Next came some road construction and the long hill into the town of Lethbridge.

In the car, I sat behind the driver, Paul. Erina sat by the other window, and Marisha sat in the middle of the backseat. Of course, Helen sat up front in the passenger seat. She was playing backseat driver, and Paul was paying a bit of attention to her.

All of a sudden, there was a narrowing of the road's lane on our side. Helen yelled, "Watch that big truck!"

He was in our lane, trying to pass another truck going uphill. Marisha was screaming, as I was. Then everything went blank.

All I could feel was pain. I knew the truck had hit us. There were groans and crying all around me; I did not know whether some of it was me. I opened my eyes, and all I saw was blood. I could not put my arms to my face. I must have blacked out. In the distance, I heard what sounded like the sirens. The police—or was it an ambulance?

I thought I heard someone say, "Not him, he is dead."

Then again: "Get the back ones first."

Is this a dream, or what? I thought.

That was all I remembered, until a few days later, when I was awakened by Annie, my sister, and Annette hovering around me. "Oh, dear. Where am I?" I asked. Then I felt and saw nothing.

It was over a week before I was aware of my surroundings. I was told I had been in a car accident. I was not to talk; my gums were missing on the left side, and plastic surgery was done to replace them. My left cheek was not yet replaced, because my cheekbone was shattered and needed an operation. I could lift one arm to feel the other hand. All I was aware of was a tube in the other arm. The nurses did not want me to move.

After what seemed like many days, Annie and Annette were both there. When I focused on them, I recognized their voices.

A man told me he was the doctor, and he told me not to talk. I was heavily sedated and would not remember things. One of my eyes was all right, but the other had been replaced in the socket, and they were not sure about it being all right; it was all bandaged. The cheekbone was shattered and removed by the doctors, and I'd had plastic surgery done on my cheek, as well as the gums, which were healing beautifully, I was told. That was a joke, adding to my nose. Nothing was beautiful.

"Quit kidding me," I said. Then darkness came again, and I had no memory.

I lost track of time. Annie and Annette were by my side and stayed until the next day.

There stood a kindly gentleman. It was a distant relative whom I did not know. He told me I had two broken collarbones, and my left arm was broken in two places. Both of my legs were broken, the left one above the knee, and the right one below the knee. I had a sprained wrist in my right arm, and I also had cracked ribs. The doctors were not considering putting me in casts, because I would be one big cast.

Larri, the gentleman, said he lived in Lethbridge and had a lot of Hudderite friends, one of who was a chiropractor. He talked to the doctor attending me and said he would keep me out of pain.

Larri said, "I will sneak the chiropractor into the hospital and have him set your broken bones. That will be your only chance to heal most. Do not say no." All I did was nod my head, and the nodding caused a lot of pain. I again blacked out.

That evening, I was told they were moving me to a private room for the night. Annie and Annette left after telling me they would see me in the morning.

I was all alone. This was how it all would end. I did

not expect to see tomorrow. The doctor came in, and I learned his name was Dr. Lerner. He said he would give me a shot, and I would sleep until the morning. I thought, *This is it. The end.* I tried to smile, I think.

As the needle took effect, my poem ran through my head. "Oh, woe is me. How bad can this be?"

Recovery?

The next morning, I did wake up. Annie and Annette came to say good-bye. I did not want them to leave me like this, but they had to go home.

Larri and another gentleman, James Chatters, were by my bedside. They told me they had been there in the evening, after I got my nightly shot from Dr. Lerner.

While I slept, James set all my broken bones. The left shoulder bone was a hard job and may not be quite as well set as the rest, because there were a few small shards of bone that would need a great deal of tender loving care, and lots of massaging. All the bones needed a lot of care in the future. I needed a lot of pain medication, which Dr. Lerner prescribed for me.

As far as doctors and nurses were concerned, James had not been at the hospital, now or ever. Both of the men left.

I was alone again. I was in pain, but I was not really in pain; it seemed like I was elsewhere, looking down on myself.

Erina was all right, and she was going home. Her son came to get her. She came to say good-bye to me.

She told me Paul had died on impact with the truck.

Helen had died at the scene of the accident. Marisha had died a week later, in this hospital. Their children had arranged for their funerals at home.

Erina and I survived, and here I was, with no family of my own. Why was I still hanging on?

I spoke for the first time, and I said good-bye to her, wishing her the best. She said she would see me in a few weeks, adding, "You will be going home real soon."

Was I feeling sorry for myself? Was everything going to be all right, and would I see her in a few weeks?

I was all bandaged and had splints and tape on both legs, shoulders, and arms. My shoulder blades were both bandaged. Dr. Lerner had x-rays done on all my broken bones, and he hummed as he looked at them. Later he told me he was very pleased to see how well I'd healed. There was no mention of the chiropractor.

He told me he had gotten ahold of my doctor in Castlegar. He would send him the results and what medication I would have to take, as well as all the x-rays. I could possibly go home in two weeks' time.

Home Again

Annette was informed about me coming home. Johnnie and his wife, Nell, were to pick me up in Nelson at the train station. An ambulance staff put me on the train. I was on a stretcher but in a sitting position. I saw a lot of familiar places through a mist because I was on a strong pain medication. The next thing I knew, I was in Nelson.

Johnnie walked onto the train and lifted me up effortlessly; he was so strong and gentle. He put me in the backseat of his car, with pillows all around me. I could not move even if I tried. Soon I was in my own bedroom surrounded by Annie, Annette, Nellie, and a few of our neighbors. Even the dog sneaked in to give me a lick before he was shooed out the door.

That evening, Dr. Rruebsaut, who had taken Dr. Gaeyton's place when the elder had retired and left the area, gave me pills to take and a shot for pain. He told me to have a bite to eat and try get some sleep and took all the papers I had from the Lethbridge hospital.

The next afternoon, he came to see me again. Annie was there and was worried about me. He gave her instructions: a few gentle massage instructions to be done on my sore spots. There would be more sore areas when the splints and bandages came off in four weeks.

Ian was coming home on the weekend, so Michael drove Annie home. She promised to come back soon, which she did, and she was a great nurse. We had many laughs and reminisced about old times. My heart was not into laughter, however.

She lost weight and told me it was deliberate. She told me she had diabetes, and she needed to lose weight. Here I was, feeling sorry for myself. I told myself I had to snap out of it. Life did go on. Eventually I realized there was a reason for everything, even for me. I was beginning to see that for some reason, I was meant to be on this earth, and to go on.

A few weeks went by quickly. I walked with the help of crutches and went to see Dr. Rruebsaut. He took x-rays. The left collarbone needed rebreaking and a cast for six to eight weeks. I told him I knew a chiropractor in Hills and would like to try him. Michael took me to Annie's, and Velda went with me to Hills to see the chiropractor.

Velda did not make a good nurse and would cringe from pain that I felt. She panicked when I fainted as the chiropractor rebroke my collarbone. Here I was, in a new splint, bandaged and taped again. Good thing I had a lot of pain pills.

Trip to Victoria

I had to get new dentures. I went to a dentist and had impressions done. The teeth were ready in a week because we had a dental mechanic in Castlegar, and they fit perfectly.

My bones started to heal. I was able to walk with a cane built by Papa. It was short like me, and he'd told me that when he'd given it to me many years ago. I told him I did not need a cane.

His reply was "You will when you get old."

I guess I was old. It seemed I got old all at once.

It was as if all my life had been illness and medical problems. Why, why, why?

Here I went again: "Woe is me."

I had a problem with my left eye. The glasses surprisingly did not get broken during the accident, and they did not seem to correct the issue. The cheek was beautiful and smooth, and the Lethbridge doctors had done an excellent job on my gums and cheek. I could not see everything. Things did not line up. I saw double objects, one higher than the other. Dr. Lemoy sent me to an ophthalmologist, who referred me to Dr. Nord in Victoria.

How was I going to go there? Velda took time off from work and got Annette to come with us. Soon we were off to Vancouver, on the ferry and heading to Victoria. The nieces were very attentive. We stayed in nice hotels, ate breakfast in their nice restaurants. I had boiled eggs, toast, and coffee. I still did not eat meat.

That morning we went to see Dr. Nord. After a checkup, he knew what was wrong, and he had been in touch with the doctors in Lethbridge Hospital. The doctor was told when I was brought into the hospital, the eye was hanging on the injured cheek. When the cheek and gums were fixed, the eye was also fixed and put into place, but a bit lower than the right eye. This created double vision.

Now that everything was healed, the eye would have to be measured against the other, operated on, and lifted to match the left one. He said he had scheduled an appointment two weeks from this day.

I said, "In the meantime, we are going to see Victoria." The girls took me for high tea at the Empress—too expensive to my liking, but very enjoyable.

We drove to Anne Hathaway's Cottage. We drove along the waterfront and the harbor. We went to the parliament buildings, stayed an extra day, and went to the wax museum.

We went to Buchart Garden. I'd never seen so many flowers in my entire life. The girls took turns pushing me in the wheelchair. If they were as tired as I was, then I was sure they were exhausted, but I never heard a complaint. They did not mind, because it was easier than me walking.

I would never have kept up with them. We all slept well after a great dinner at a beautiful restaurant.

The next morning, we again went to breakfast. I told the girls I was not hungry, but Velda said she would order for me. "I can order my own boiled egg" was my reply. I did not want the smell of meat on my breakfast, in case the eggs were fried on the same grill as bacon.

I got the surprise of my life. The waitress set a beautiful china plate in front of me. On it was a great big waffle with a layer of fresh strawberries, covered with fluffy whipped cream. It seemed like too much food for me, but I ate the whole thing. It was delicious!

We got on the ferry to go home. I must admit, I had put on a bit of weight. The car parked on the extended deck, and we were close to the railing on the driver's side, so I had extra room to get out. However, the car next to us parked closer to us. Velda said, "Get out."

I could not get out. Her car was a two-door, and she and I were in the front seat, with Annette in the back. Annette had to exit through my side of the front door. So there we sat.

Finally Velda said, "Roll down the window, open the door, and get out."

I rolled down the window and opened the door, but I could not get out.

By then the girls were having a good laugh at my expense. It was not funny. They were laughing so hard that they could not tell me to lift my fat tummy above, window level, because the car had no window frames, and get out. I finally did it.

"There I am, out. How are you two getting out?" I said.

They were both taller than me but skinny as rails, so there was no problem.

The car ferry was in motion. We walked up a set of stairs, and the girls were still laughing. I was sort of angry. I would not let them hold my arm to make sure I did not fall. Annette insisted on helping me up on the stool at the counter because all the chairs and tables were taken.

She and Velda grabbed both of my arms and boosted me up on the stool. While doing this, Velda stepped on a coffee creamer someone had dropped, and it squirted on a lady's beautiful purse, which she had set on the floor by her chair.

It was my turn to giggle. We three were laughing like crazy. Velda finally stopped laughing, took some serviettes over to the lady, and asked if she could wipe the coffee cream off the purse. She was embarrassed, but she could not wipe the smile off her face. Good thing the lady was cordial about the whole thing! All was well, and we had a lot of patrons of the cafe laughing.

It was an odd thing to remember for an old lady. I'd aged the last few months. However, I also had a better outlook on life.

The girls were really good to me. Now here I was, grumpy again.

I let Velda order all my meals for the rest of that trip. I was too stubborn to admit they were all good, and there was no meat.

Well Again

Two weeks later, Annette and cousin Aylla drove me to Victoria for the eye surgery. The operation went well, and I could see again, with no more double vision.

Dr. Nord told me he could get his friend, a plastic surgeon, to operate on my nose. It would look like my smooth cheek. I refused him and his kindness. He could not understand why I would not agree to this because it was not going to cost me anything.

My reply was "People stared at me most of my life, and now they have sort of quit. They will stare and gossip again, if I get a new nose after all these years."

He told me to think about this. I did, and I decided, "No, I cannot. I have changed. I no longer think of myself. I thought there were many people who need work done on them, and they are younger than me. I have lived to reach my seventies. Some people need surgery to live, and I will not be selfish. I will not take up space in the hospitals, or the doctor's time."

He telephoned me, and I thanked him from the bottom of my heart for giving me back my vision.

I spent the rest of the winter at Velda and Pedro's new, unfinished house. Dasha was a good child who was very caring and amusing. She and I even learned to do the Cossack dance, with a few *oops* when we fell down on our behinds.

Velda was at work. Pedro was doing construction jobs and was home occasionally. I had a bedroom of my own. They took me to Spokane, to a skating show. "I could skate, if I tried," I said. Dasha laughed at that one. She took me shopping, riding up and down escalators, and we had fun. They took me to movies. I spent an enjoyable winter there.

We lost Nellie. She had diabetes, did not eat properly, and suffered for a while. She was hospitalized for a few weeks and lost out. That was not enjoyable, and we all missed her.

Annie was suffering from diabetes, and she had a heart attack and cirrhosis of the liver. She spent months in the hospital, went home, and then had to go back to the hospital to get fluid drained from her lungs.

That summer Velda, Pedro, and Dasha went to the expo in Montreal, in their new trailer. Things were not good between them. I heard Pedro was seeing someone else. There was a divorce that January. Annie was in the hospital three months, and she did not have a clue about their divorce. She passed away in March and did not live to see her retirement. Ian was devastated, and he still lived on the farm.

Velda was working three jobs because their divorce was bad. She had the house to pay for and no car. Michael gave her his old car, and it was a gas-guzzler that burned as much oil as gas. Velda never complained. I took Dasha home on weekends, and we enjoyed having her. Whereas

I'd learned to speak English when I was young, she wanted to learn to speak Russian.

She went to Saskatchewan with Alosha and me. She read all the signs for us and told us where to turn, where to stop, and what we had to see. It was enjoyable. Every year she was more independent. She grew up too fast.

Michael got a girlfriend, finally. She moved in with him at his newly built house. He was so in debt that he was losing all our Pass Creek property. He had a mortgage on everything. Alex and I went to see the manager of the credit union. He let us take over the mortgage, but we had to get Michael's' name off the title. That was all right because we still owned two-thirds of it. Michael was very angry, but he signed it over. His girlfriend was also angry, and as they left, they packed up everything, even stuff that was not theirs. The last anyone had heard from them, they were seen drinking in a pub in Winnipeg.

Moving Again

Alosha and I moved into the new house, painted it, fixed up everything, and added a garage. Alex, as we all called him, was still working for the school board but was ready to retire. He sold the property across the road. The hillside property belonged to me, and I sold that. We paid off the mortgage on the Pass Creek property.

Our dog got run over. The cat missed him, and then she too disappeared. We were sad for a long time and missed them.

Alosha was seeing a lady friend. I wished he would marry and be happy. He told me he worried about me. The lady friend and he broke up, so I told him to find another friend. His comment was that he was too old to get saddled with anyone.

I told him not to worry, because I was getting old and tired. He certainly did not have to feel responsible for me. It was time I moved into a seniors home, like the doctor had suggested. It would not be a bad idea.

Velda would come up see us occasionally. She had a new boyfriend, but we did not much care for him. Dasha was getting grown up and was thinking about the university in Vancouver. We did not see her as often because she had her friends.

Ian moved into Castlegar.

Johnnie bought his farm. He and Nell had three children: two boys, and the last was a girl with reddish-blonde hair. They divorced, and Nell took up nursing. Johnnie worked construction work and was away most of the time.

Alosha and I finally decided to sell the Pass Creek property. I was going to move into a seniors place, but Annette had found a new husband since Mike had died. Would you believe it? When I saw him, it was Malcomb from Creston—the young lad who'd cheated me out of strawberry cups and given them to Natashka.

They moved to Kimberly to look after Annette's daughter's motel. They wanted us to buy Annette's house in Kinnaird. It was the right size for us, so we gave her a hefty bit of money as a down payment and moved in. I did not go to a seniors home like I wanted.

In the spring, I seeded a hot bed and got beautiful cucumbers and tomatoes. The tomatoes we transplanted into the garden. I was very proud of it until I fell down trying to weed it. I decided it was time I went into a seniors home, because I did not need a garden or a house to look after. When I suggested it to Alosha, he was very sad. I felt sorry for him because he had no one. He told me he needed me to talk to him. All my relatives were his too. He helped with a lot of things, including all the outside chores. He even did the laundry because he did not feel I should go downstairs.

There I was, changing my mind again. Here, I was still cleaning house, doing laundry, and weeding gardens. I did not need that at age eighty-seven.

My First Plane Ride

That fall, Dasha went to the University of British Columbia. She stayed at the dorms in the beginning, and later she shared an apartment. I did not see much of her or her mother that winter and spring.

In the summer, when Dasha was home, she popped in occasionally. She grew up to be a fine young lady and had a job in Vancouver. I did not see much of her. Everyone was busy, including me.

Come August, Dasha decided on her own apartment in Vancouver. Velda was flying down to apartment hunt.

They had a ticket bought for me. "On an airplane? For me?" I asked. That was something I had not considered! I was scared because I had never flown anywhere in my eighty-eight years. I was excited that they would even consider taking me.

I was told to pack a few days' worth of clothes, and not to forget my meds—I had a lot of them. I was so excited. I wanted to run and tell all my neighbors.

The day came to go to the airport. Alosha drove us, and it was just across the river. I saw it from my backyard.

The next thing I knew, I was buckled in my seat,

with Velda beside me. I was actually on a plane! I did not remember the ride because I was so excited.

Dasha picked us up at the Vancouver airport with her little orange car. It was so cute! We apartment hunted for two days. She finally found one, and of course I had to go see it. It was in a good neighborhood with a nice landlady. It passed my inspection, as if that mattered. We had a good laugh about that.

Velda promised to take me to California someday, on a longer plane ride. My would have never dreamed I would go on a plane ride.

More Pain

Annette came over from Kimberly to collect her monthly payments. She hinted that maybe we should move there too, and she would sell this house. How could *she* sell it? It was sold to us!

The doctor gave me some pills for my nerves, and I thought I was getting addicted to them. My stomach was bothering me so bad, and I lost so much weight. I told the doctor, who sent me for x-rays. I was sent to the Trail Hospital and had scans done on my stomach. There were more tests because the doctors were worried. I was down to ninety-nine pounds, and even for my small size, that was bad.

I'd spent so much time in hospitals, all my life. Here I went one more time. Finally, they told me I needed an operation, but I had to put on a few pounds. By then, I could not even keep down water. Velda came with Dasha and her friend Jannie. We all cried.

The oncologist came in to talk to me, and the girls left. The nice doctor explained to me that I was too thin and weak from not eating for the last ten days. He wanted to know if I still wanted to go ahead with the cancer operation. The doctor said they would have to make a large cut in the lower part of my stomach. Then they'd remove at least twenty-four inches of the intestine, checking to make sure there was no more cancer, because it may have spread. He explained everything very thoroughly and carefully, to make sure I understood. It was a fifty-fifty chance that I would not make it.

I closed my eyes and thought, *Have I anything to lose?*

I said to Dr. Standton, "I am eighty-eight years old. Maybe I will die, because it is time for me to go."

He did not want me to talk like that.

I also thought of all the pain I'd endured so many times in my life. That came to mind, and I said, "No, I do not want more pain, and someone else will need this bed. Someone who is younger than me, with a family that needs them."

All at once, the curtain moved. Velda burst in; she had been listening to everything. Both the doctor and I were surprised. "She will have the operation," Velda said. "We will not let her die. She has not been to California with me! I promised to take her to Disneyland. You have to operate as soon as you can. She still has so much to do. She has much to see." She went on and on.

There I lay, trying to be brave. It was decided for me. I could not die from the operation.

The next morning, I was prepared for the operation. Velda was there, and she kissed me and said, "See you later. I have to go to work, to earn enough money to take us both to California."

I said good-bye.

Her reply was "Not good-bye. See you tonight."

I was wheeled into the operating room. That was all I remembered.

After a few days, I came to some awareness. Everything was a blur. I remembered Velda, Dasha, and her friend Jannie. They could not stay away.

Every day I felt better, and soon I was able to get up, which I did. Weak as I was, I had to walk. Then it was time to take the bandages off. I had clamps and stitches across my stomach. That hurt, and I had to take it easy for a while.

It was soon time to go home. Arrangements were made for someone to look after me, cook my meals, clean the house, and do all the other necessities. Lena was a very nice lady and excellent cook, and she cleaned every nook and cranny. She helped me in and out of the tub and the bed, and she took me for walks. I grew to love her very much. She was so kind, patient, and caring.

It was odd to be a lady of leisure. I even got to watch the soap operas on television in the afternoons! Alosha had purchased a new colored TV. Life was not bad after all. I healed well and quickly.

Lena stayed on. She came in the morning, cleaned, and made sure all our meals were taken care of for all day. I no longer needed her to help me into the bed or the tub. I still did not lift anything.

I went to physiotherapy and was told to exercise. In addition to my exercise from the auto accident, I did more. The doctors were impressed at how well I was doing.

I felt a lot better physically and mentally. Annette stayed away for a while, and I was happy about that. Then one day, I walked outside to find a surveyor in the backyard. The back lot had been sold, he said. The survey pegs were in my garden—it was no longer ours.

There was an excavator digging a basement for a new house on the lot next door.

Time to Pack

Alosha and I went to town for coffee, and we sat in the coffee shop. The door flew open, and in came Velda in her usual whirlwind fashion. She had only a half hour for lunch and asked me how I felt. My answer was "I am okay, but we still have not been to California."

She stood up without answering me and left. A few minutes later she was back. She plopped a handful of brochures in front of me and told me to look them over and decide where I wanted to go.

On her way out the door, she said she had two weeks' holidays coming, and that was when we'd go.

Five days later, we were in Vancouver. We spent a night with Dasha and then headed to the Vancouver airport. We were on a plane to Anaheim, California. Velda even thought to order my meals on the plane to be vegetarian.

I could not believe I was going on a plane again. It was so exciting! In the back of my mind, I could not forget what had happened to our back lot. I told Velda, and she was very angry with Annette. Thank goodness we were on the plane, because I could not fathom what she would have done if we were home.

Finally she said, "Forget it, and enjoy this trip."

Thanks to Velda, this was my second trip on the plane.

Soon we were in California. I'd never dreamed of this. My niece had planned everything. We went to Disneyland and went on all the rides except one; when they learned I was eighty-nine years old, they would not let us go on the Matterhorn. I walked and walked, and I got tired; only then would I let my niece get a wheelchair, and she wheeled me everywhere.

We went to Knotsberry Farm, Universal Studios, and Hollywood. We walked the sidewalk with all the actors' names. Yes, I walked it—with a cane, mind you.

Velda even took me to Tijuana, Mexico, for a day. A bunch of little kids tried to sell me some large flowers and all kinds of things.

One evening, a friend of Velda's and his wife took us sightseeing, and then we went to dinner at a posh restaurant.

My friends Alan and Marcia came to visit me. I'd babysat Alan when he was young; now he was an old man. He commented that I had not changed or aged at all.

I do not remember ever enjoying my time so much. I was very thankful that Velda had taken me. She would not let me pay for anything, and I knew how hard she'd worked to do this.

Every evening when we got back to the hotel, I did my exercises. One night I forgot, and I got up at four in the morning to do them. As I was doing my sit-ups, Velda woke up and groaned. When she found out what I was doing, I had to explain that I had done exercises almost all my life. That was why I was living so long!

That was the best time I'd ever spent away from home. Soon it was over, and I was back in Vancouver, and soon to go home again.

Kimberley? Why?

I got home too soon—or was it too late? Alosha met me at the door, and he looked very sad. He told me Annette had informed him that she'd sold the house we were in, the house we'd made a sufficient down payment on, the house we made monthly payments on. This was the house I had grown to call home.

"How did she do this? It was our house," I said.

"No," he said. "We made all those payments and deposit, and we trusted her, but we did not sign any papers that stated it was ours. She did not give us any receipts for our deposit, or for any of the payments."

She'd sold it. She wanted us to move into the motel they were looking after in Kimberley. I was to live with Annette and Malcomb, and Alex had a room in the basement.

I did not sleep all night. In the morning, I phoned Velda. She came to the house before she went to work. She was very angry and said we could get a place at the seniors villa.

She phoned Annette. Annette's reply was "The house is sold, and there is nothing you can do. There are no records that they paid anything."

Velda wanted to go to a lawyer, but we wanted to keep peace with everyone. She was very angry. I'd never seen her so livid about anything. Finally she said, "Okay, we can try this, but it will not work out living with Annette and Malcomb. Alosha, if there is anything that I can do for you, let me know."

We moved to Kimberly in July. We would try our best to make things work.

In October, Velda and Sam, her new beau, came on a motorbike to visit us. When she knocked on the door in her bike helmet, covered in rain, I did not want to let them in until I finally recognized her. Annette and Malcomb were away, and we were looking after the motel.

They told us if there was anything they could do to get us out of this predicament, they would do it. We must have looked so sad, which we were. They took us out for lunch at a cafe a few doors down from us. I was ready to cry and had a lump in my throat. I could not swallow much, so most of the lunch was untouched.

Velda talked to Alex, as she often called him. He must have told her he was very unhappy. I was unhappy too, but I did not let on. The rain stopped, and soon they were on their way back to Castlegar. They had moved closer into town since we'd left the area. I wished them the best with a sad heart, but I sent them on their way.

October was a dull and dreary month, and November was worse. Alex told me he'd phoned Velda and told her to get him a place in the seniors villa, which was across the street from Velda's new house.

Before the month was over, Velda pulled a few strings with her friends. She got Alex a suite in the villa. It was one street over from her house; all she had to do was run across the street and down a flight of stairs, and she would be able to see Alex. He could also come visit any time he wanted.

He loaded his car with all his belongings. Some things Annette would not let him take, claiming he did not need them. With sad feelings, he left Kimberley, and he said I should do the same. We said our good-byes. I did not let him see me cry. To me, he was the good son I'd never had.

Velda was very angry with Annette because she had sent him to the villa with as little as possible. Velda phoned and told her to send all of his good dishes, all his stainless pots and pans, all his new bedding and good comforters, and his dress shirts. It was to be on the bus that evening. If all of Alex's belongings were not on the bus, the police would be knocking on her door.

Annette did not say anything to me, but she got boxes and started packing all of Alosha's stuff. They made the bus schedule and were there that night. He phoned me and told me what had happened.

I thought about going to a nursing home. Annette said that I would not be able to live on my own, and no one would look after me like she would. With many doubts, I stayed.

Alosha phoned often. He was happier there, and I was happy for him.

Alosha phoned at Christmas. He was having dinner with Velda, Dasha and Sam, and Sam's four children. They were there from Calgary. I wished I was with them.

I had a quiet Christmas dinner with Annette and Malcomb. He sat and frowned at me. I had a hard time swallowing because I had a lump in my throat almost all the time; I was ready to cry.

What could I do? I was not well. Everything felt sore, and my health was failing quickly. I got severe headaches, which I'd never had before. Annette took me to her doctor, but he could not find anything wrong, I got more pills from him. I think I had pills to make me sleep, and then pills to wake me up. I took pills for my constant pain.

Aileen, Annette's daughter, came to see me. She loved me. Her mother told her that she would take me take to Castlegar, drop me off at the hospital, and have my old doctor look after me there.

A few months later, she did just that. There I lay in the Castlegar hospital. I did not have a quarter to phone anyone; as a matter of fact, I did not have my purse or any identification. My old doctor came in and greeted me like he missed me. He told me he would look after me and would find a nice, comfortable seniors home.

Unknown by me, Aileen phoned Velda and told her what her mother had done to me. She would drop me off at the hospital and leave Velda's phone number as the contact. "She took her in her night clothes," Aileen said, sobbing.

Velda's hot temper was sizzling. When she came to the hospital, she was crying. She had asked me to come with her the last time she'd talked on the telephone. But I'd trusted Annette. I'd pretended everything was all right. So here I was. At least I was taken care of.

I later learned from Alosha that Velda had called him over to her house and told him what had happened. She phoned around Castlegar and found Annette. She told her to come over right away to discuss this matter like a civil person—like Annette should have done in the first place.

She came over and, in a not very civil way, according to Alosha. There was a lot of bad language used.

Annette and Malcomb had used us. Annette was crying. Alosha was very sad because he'd treated her like a real sister. Of course, she blamed this on Malcomb. But she was there too. I heard all of this from Alosha. When I talked to Velda, she said, "All is okay. Do not worry; the doctor will look after you."

I did worry, because Annette had my savings from the bank. I did not even have anything for my funeral. Alosha told me not to worry, because we would manage.

I took a turn for the worse. I did not remember if I'd brushed my teeth. I forgot to comb my hair. Velda went out and bought all the necessary things that Annette had not brought with me.

Finally, Annette sent some of my belongings I would need at the hospital. She sent my sleeping gowns and my dressing gown. Did she not know I got up and dressed every day? Good thing Velda was here. She bought me a bunch of new things.

Last Days I Remember

My doctor came in one morning. I had been in the Castlegar hospital about five months. He told me I was moving to a nursing home in Nelson, where they would take good care of me.

My memory was bad. I do remember Velda visiting, and Alosha visiting. Velda told me Dotty and John came to see me too.

I asked, "Why did Nellie and Annie not come to visit?"

Oh, dear—they had passed away years ago. I seemed to have outlived everyone.

Nelson? Yes, Nelson!

There I was, in a beautiful room, overlooking a flower garden. I stood by the window and admired it. Velda came to see me on her days off. She brought me new clothes, because she wanted me to look nice. She brought me candy and chocolate bars, and anything I asked for. One day I did not recognize her. How did I not recognize her?

Four weeks before my ninety-fifth birthday, I fell and broke my hip. I ended up getting operated on again and had the hip replaced with a metal one. I could not walk, so I was confined to a wheelchair. Even if I was able to walk, I could not remember where I was, where I was going, or how to get there.

Some days I would not remember who I was.

Velda brought a large cake that was enough for all the patients on the whole floor, and all my relatives came to visit, bringing goodies for my ninety-fifth birthday.

When Velda wheeled me into the sitting room, I recognized Dotty and Marcia. Marcia had had a stroke a few years previously that had paralyzed her left side. There was Lena, my caretaker; Elsie, our old neighbor; and another lady whom I recognized but could not remember her name (it was Marjie, a niece of mine). Annette had the nerve to come. I remembered her, but God help me, I looked right past her and pretended she was not there. There were all the people from this floor of the nursing home, and they sang "Happy Birthday" to me.

I remembered this day and marveled. It was my ninety-fifth birthday.

How had I lived this long? I could not remember other things. Maybe it was just as well. It was time to forgive and forget. Forgive what? Forget what?

I was so tired. Everything was a blur. I ate when I was told. I drank when I was able to swallow. Someone fed me, and I chewed and swallowed when I could. Someone bathed me, put clean clothes on me, and made my bed. Sometimes I was happy, I think. Had this all happened, or was I just dreaming? My memory was not good.

I think some of my relatives came to see me. I think Velda came to see me, and I think she held my hand.

I could no longer decide whether it was real or just a dream. I did not know or remember anything.

Each day ran into the next. I tried to be nice. Sometimes I was mean. I remember being uncooperative. I think I was, but I really did not know.

Most of the time, I slept. My whole body ached. I hoped for sleep—eternal sleep. I prayed.

Velda Said

Aunt Mary lived to be ninety-seven years old. She died in Mount St. Francis, the nursing home in Nelson, British Columbia, on October 3, 1985, of heart failure, or Alzheimer's, or maybe old age and dementia, according to the doctors.

She was laid to rest at Pass Creek Cemetery. She did not want a marker on her grave. God rest her soul.

I am writing this as I often told her I would do. As I was growing up, I made notes on scraps of paper as I listened to the many stories she told me over the years. I promised I would write this, but she never believed I would.

This is written for all her relatives to read. I may not know them all.

This is written for all her friends—and she had a great many of them.

This is written for all you people who saw her and were curious about what happened to her.

This is written to all the people who were mean to her. Hopefully none are around to read this. Those who were mean must be real old.

This is written to all the people who were kind to her during her trying years, when she needed them the most. If you are reading this, you will know who you are. Thank you.

This is written to all the doctors. Many of you are not around now, but a few are here still. If you read this, you will remember her. Thank you.

This is written for everyone who reads this book. Enjoy.

The End

About the Author

Vee Konkin was born and raised in the southern interior of British Columbia, Canada, where she went to school, worked, and retired. When she was younger, she spent a lot of time with her aunt, Mankiya. She kept notes from their conversations in a little wooden box and told her that she would one day write her story. This is her first book.

Printed in the United States
By Bookmasters